I Remember
BUD WILKINSON

Other Books in the I Remember Series

I Remember
BUD WILKINSON

Personal Memories and Anecdotes
about an Oklahoma Sooners Legend
as Told by the People and Players
Who Knew Him

MIKE TOWLE

Cumberland House
Nashville, Tennessee

Published by
    Cumberland House Publishing, Inc.
    431 Harding Industrial Drive
    Nashville, TN 37211
    www.cumberlandhouse.com

Cover design by Gore Studio, Inc.

Library of Congress Cataloging-in-Publication Data has been applied for

    Towle, Mike.
        I Remember B ud Wilkinson : Personal memories and anecdotes
        about an Oklahoma Sooners legend as told by the people and play-
        ers who knew him / Mike Towle
            p.   cm.
        Includes index.
        ISBN 1-58182-301-0 (alk. paper)

Printed in Canada
1 2 3 4 5 6 7—07 06 05 04 03 02

Contents

To Mercy Belle

PREFACE

Like many baby boomers weaned on sports during the sixties and seventies, I really didn't know who Bud Wilkinson was or where he had come from—what his background had been. All I knew was that he was the guy with the quiet, soothing voice who did color commentary for ABC Television's coverage of college football for many years, starting in the mid-sixties.

Wilkinson was the calm in the middle of a production storm comprised of gripping play-by-play commentary and sideline sidebars, splashes of color, quick-hitting camera shots over the stadium, and a screenful of graphics. Bud didn't talk a whole lot, but he seemed to be smiling all the time on those occasions when his face was on camera. His game commentary was spare but refreshingly specific, enhanced by the movement of small board pieces that represented play formations and X's and O's. Bud Wilkinson was like a favorite uncle I didn't meet until I was ten years old, not fully realizing where he had been and what he had done before entering my life.

It was only later, about the time that the NFL's Saint Louis Cardinals picked Wilkinson out of the blue to be their new head coach, that I came to appreciate Wilkinson's own success on the football field. He had played at the University of Minnesota during the 1930s, first as a guard and then as a quarterback, as part of a Golden Gophers team that won consecutive national championships in 1934, 1935, and 1936.

Those were fertile times for rich football success in the Land of a Thousand Lakes. Meanwhile, just hundreds of miles away, the plains of Oklahoma were under assault by dust storms that covered most of the state, devastated crops, and nearly broke the spirits of more than a million Oklahomans. Minnesota and Oklahoma might just as well have been a million miles apart, and it took a native-born son from the former to emerge as a savior for the latter.

That man was Bud Wilkinson, who from 1947 to 1963 built, sustained, and guided a college football dynasty that produced three national championships, four unbeaten seasons among eight seasons of ten or more victories, thirty-six All-Americans, one Heisman Trophy winner (Billy Vessels, in 1952), and a seventeen-year mark of 145-29-4 (.826). Perhaps the only thing that keeps Wilkinson from being ranked above the best of the best among college football coaches—among the likes of Bear Bryant, Woody Hayes, Bobby Bowden, and Joe Paterno—is the relatively brief duration of his college coaching career. Wilkinson was forty-six when he retired as Oklahoma coach, while Bryant, Hayes, Bowden, and Paterno were still coaching well into their sixties or even seventies.

After retiring as Sooners coach following the 1963 season, Wilkinson embarked on a career second half that included a run for the U.S. Senate, serving as head of the President's

Council on Youth Fitness, television work as a college football analyst, consulting with political leaders inside the Washington, D.C., Beltway, being involved with various business ventures and charities, and coming out of coaching retirement briefly to coach the Cardinals. There always seemed to be a lot going on in Wilkinson's life, which could have been expected of someone who loved sports and competition and had taken the time to earn a master's degree in English and later served as a naval officer during World War II.

I Remember Bud Wilkinson is a collection of numerous firsthand stories, anecdotes, insights, and commentary about Wilkinson by dozens of people who knew him well in one capacity or another. This is not a birth-to-death biography filled with dates and details; it is an oral history of an American icon whose career touched sports, politics, business, and media.

A book of this sort is possible only with the cooperation of many people willing to share personal memories that sometimes aren't easy to give up. There were a number of people contacted for this book that declined to be interviewed, but I am thankful for the following who did contribute, either in face-to-face interviews or over the telephone: Claude Arnold, David Baker, Don Brown, Bob Burris, Jerry Cross, Eddie Crowder, John Derr, Bob Ewbank, Bill Flemming, Curt Gowdy, Jim Hanifan, Jimmy Harris, Jim Hart, Keith Jackson, Buddy Leake, Geoff Mason, Pat O'Neal, Jim Otis, Ara Parseghian, Joe Rector, John Reddell, J. D. Roberts, Darrell Royal, Andy Sidaris, Lee Allen Smith, Barry Switzer, Jerry Tubbs, and Roger Wehrli.

I am also grateful to the Oklahoma University Football Media Relations Department for their help, hospitality, and generosity with time and materials while I was researching files and photos for this book. They were especially generous in allowing me to pick and use photos for this book. Ditto for the Arizona Cardinals public relations staff. Thanks, too, to Ron

Pitkin, John Mitchell, and the entire Cumberland House crew for sharing an interest in publishing this book as the latest in the *I Remember* series.

My wife, Holley, and son, Andrew, were super troopers in giving me plenty of room timewise to complete this project, which involved a lot of work in a short amount of time.

In closing, I thank my Savior, Jesus Christ, for His saving grace and never-ending wisdom and guidance.

I Remember
BUD WILKINSON

FROM DUST BOWL TO SUGAR BOWL

Bud Wilkinson didn't invent winning football at the University of Oklahoma. He resurrected it. Forty-one years before Wilkinson made his way to Norman, Oklahoma, a gent by the name of Bennie Owen had begun a twenty-two-year era that would produce 122 Oklahoma victories against 54 losses and 16 ties. Owen didn't spend his career bumping Knute Rockne out of the sports headlines, but his teams did accomplish some memorable things. Four of his squads went undefeated; eight times he had teams lay a hundred or more points on overmatched opponents. Eat your heart out, Barry "Half-a-Hundred" Switzer.

The Owen years were ancient history by the thirties, however; the memories for the most part buried under windblown dust like some irretrievable Indiana Jones artifacts. Once a land rich for farming, Oklahoma was devastated by a drought and terrible dust storms that dried up the soil and blew it away. That coincided with the Great Depression following the stock-market crash of 1929. Hundreds of thousands of Oklahomans packed up and migrated west in search of work, their trials and tribulations becoming the basis for John Steinbeck's best-selling novel *The Grapes of Wrath*, which was made into a movie. If you could put a face on the Oklahoma of the 1930s, it would look an awful lot like Henry Fonda.

⚬〰〰〰⚬

The Grapes of Wrath came out in 1939. Then came World War II. It was a miserable time for many Oklahomans who were genuinely "dustitute" on one hand, humiliated on the other by what they perceived as inaccurate stereotypes described by Steinbeck. Enough was enough. In 1946, Oklahoma University President Dr. George Cross met with the school's board of regents to discuss ways to fight back against and conquer the bad PR, looking for a quick way to jump-start state pride and restore a sense of self-esteem. Cross suggested that the way out was through football.

So in 1946, Cross set out to bring football excellence back to Oklahoma, figuring his school would be as good a place as any in the state to take that lead. The search was on to find a head coach who could not only go toe to toe with the likes of Notre Dame's Frank Leahy and West Point's Red Blaik, but also have the ready-made connections to corral dozens of football-playing servicemen who could come to Norman and give the Sooners an instant veteran feel. Their first pick for an interview was a former North Carolina and Iowa Pre-Flight head coach named Jim Tatum. He said he would come only if he were allowed to bring along one of his protégés, a certain tall, handsome, and curly-blond-haired Adonis who would end up impressing the search committee more than Tatum.

The new Oklahoma coach was young, handsome, and about to embark on a seventeen-year adventure that saw Oklahoma football elevated to national prominence.

Tatum got the job and stayed for a year, leading the Sooners to an 8-3 season before bolting to Maryland, leaving the reins to his tagalong protégé, Bud Wilkinson. It was Wilkinson whom the OU board had been most impressed with during the interviews with Tatum, and Wilkinson didn't let them down. He took over in 1947 at the age of thirty-one and had the Sooners in the Sugar Bowl by his second season. The Sooners won their last ten games of the 1948 season to start a winning streak that would eventually reach thirty-one.

❧

Pat O'Neal, *a native of Ada, located about sixty miles southeast of Norman, was one of hundreds of young men raised in Oklahoma who after high school or the service made a beeline to Norman to play football for Bud Wilkinson. O'Neal played for the Sooners from 1951 through 1954, and as a native son he knew well what Oklahoma football meant for a state that had been beaten down during the depressing days of the Dust Bowl:*

5

To understand Oklahoma football and its place in state history, you've got to go back to World War II and the days when Oklahoma was the Dust Bowl. University president Dr. George Cross wrote a book about restoring pride in the state, and school administrators felt the fastest way to do that was to rebuild the football program into one of national prominence. This was right after the war, and the idea was to hire a good football coach who had coached during the war and would know where all the good players were. They were going to be coming out of the service. So they hired Jim Tatum, who happened to have this fellow named Bud Wilkinson tag along with him for the interview and, subsequently, a spot on the coaching staff.

Tatum stayed one year (going 8-3, before leaving to take the head job at Maryland), and then Bud took over a program that was made up of a bunch of veterans and some young punks right out of high school. I was in high school at that time. There was no televised football in those days or any football coaches' television shows; all you had was radio. In the fall of 1951 I arrived in Norman, Oklahoma, and there were still some veterans there. The atmosphere of the thing was such that authority was an accepted fact. Whoever was in charge was, in fact, in charge. Bud Wilkinson was a stern disciplinarian and what he said was gospel. In all the years I knew him, I never heard him raise his voice or lay a hand on anybody. I never saw him do anything of a personal nature, except you had better do what he said. He was one of the gentlest people I ever knew.

❧

*A generation after Wilkinson built one of college football's greatest dynasties, **Barry Switzer** stepped in as Sooners coach, although by then, the early seventies, he was a student of Oklahoma football history:*

Oklahoma was pure Americana in those days. In putting an emphasis on the school's football program and its growth, Dr. Cross made the famous statement: "I want a school that the football team can be proud of," and he wasn't trying to be funny or sarcastic. George Cross knew the importance of football after the war. Oklahoma had an inferiority complex, and then there was *The Grapes of Wrath* and all that stuff. The Dust Bowl image. The school president said we needed to take some pride in something, and the quickest way to do that was to build a winning football program. And that was his goal. They brought in Jim Tatum, but the man they really wanted was Bud Wilkinson.

⚬⚬⚬

At the same time that Tatum and then Wilkinson were picking up the mantle to carry Oklahoma football to new heights, a young radio play-by-play announcer by the name of **Curt Gowdy** *was likewise getting a start to a career that would make him a sports legend in his own right. Gowdy's first full-time job as a sports announcer was calling Sooners football, starting in 1946 and continuing until 1949. Gowdy offers some background on those early days of the rise of Oklahoma football:*

Bud and Jim Tatum had been assistant coaches at Iowa Pre-Flight under Don Faurot, who had put in the Split-T offense at Missouri. When Jim and Bud came to Oklahoma, they brought some service guys in with them. It was wide open in those days: everybody had a campus full of players.

My opening game doing radio play-by-play for the Sooners was Oklahoma-Army in New York (in 1946). The Army team, the Black Knights of the Hudson, were probably the most-publicized team ever, with (Doc) Blanchard and (Glenn) Davis, among others. A station in Oklahoma City had hired me and I

Bud was welcomed by everyone at Oklahoma eager to see football success.

OKLAHOMA UNIVERSITY FOOTBALL MEDIA RELATIONS OFFICE

came down from Cheyenne, Wyoming. I was really ecstatic about this being my first game and getting a chance to watch Army play.

It was one of the most beautiful September days that you've ever seen. Blanchard was hurt and didn't play, so Oklahoma was able to kick them all over the field. In fact, Glenn Davis had minus-twenty-seven yards rushing that day, that's how bad it was. But that's not the whole story. Davis caught a pass running backwards for a touchdown; they blocked a punt for a touchdown; and they returned an Oklahoma fumble ninety-six yards for a touchdown. Even though Oklahoma outplayed Army that day, the Black Knights ended up winning, 21-7.

ᏩᎢᎢᎢᏀ

*As of 2002 **Keith Jackson** remained a college football broadcasting icon, with his days in the broadcast booth dating back to the early fifties calling games on the West Coast. Jackson didn't do any of those early Sooners games with Wilkinson as coach, but he acquired an appreciation and knowledge of how Wilkinson had* *been prepared to take over the Sooners, which Wilkinson did before the 1947 season:*

What Bud did to achieve what he did was to change the basic philosophy of the way things were done. First off, he brought together a very good coaching staff, and this goes back to his days coaching Pre-Flight at Great Lakes Naval Station. The admiral said. "We've got to get an athletic program going here. Bud, you're a football coach, so I want you to coach the soccer team."

Bud didn't know a damn thing about soccer. Somehow, though, he got ahold of a rule book, read it in one night, I guess, and the next day he called together all of the big, ugly guys he could find and started coaching them how to play soccer. His way of coaching soccer was to tell his players that everyone goes where the ball goes except for two defensemen and the goalie. "Attack, follow the ball, and beat the hell out of anyone else trying to get to it." And they won the All-Navy Championship.

Bud brought that Oklahoma coaching staff together and then he went out to get players. He was very good in the kitchen with mama, and he was able to get together a group of people that he thought could win. And they weren't all big, brawny guys built like trucks. Take Darrell Royal, one of Bud's early star players, who came in as a little-bitty squirt. He wasn't as big as your thumb.

⚬⚬⚬⚬⚬

Curt Gowdy *recalls more from that 1946 season, which ended with the Sooners at 8-3 and Wilkinson as the new head coach after one season as an assistant under Tatum:*

They got beat at Texas, 20-13, in the third game of the season. The final gun with Oklahoma on Texas's one-yard line. Then they lost a fluke at Kansas, 16-13, in the seventh week in a driving rainstorm. Those were the only games they lost.

At the end of the season they went to the Gator Bowl in Jacksonville, going there by train. By this time Bud, who was an assistant, and I had become very close. You always get closer to an assistant than a head coach when you're covering a team like I was. Tatum was kind of a funny guy, someone you either liked or didn't like, so I would go to Bud and he would tell me a lot of stuff about what the team was trying to do—this and that. He really helped me.

We got down there to the Gator Bowl and they beat the hell out of North Carolina State, 34-13. After the game, I went down to the dressing room to congratulate them. Bud saw me and asked me what I was doing for dinner. He said, "Let's go out and get something to eat. I want to talk to you."

We went to some restaurant in Jacksonville, ate some dinner, and then were sitting around having a cup of coffee. Bud said, "Let me ask you something, Curt. What kind of a head coach do you think I'd be?" I said, "Bud, you've got one of the greatest football minds I've ever met. I haven't met a lot of them, but I know you're a very, very bright guy. In that way, I think you'd be great, but I'm not sure if you would be a good head coach or not."

"Why?"

I said, "You're too nice. You're sort of a buddy with everyone, including your players, and I think you need to be sort of a mean SOB to be a good head coach."

I'll never forget this: Bud then said, "Well, that's a shame, because they just named me head coach at Oklahoma. Jim resigned today right after the game, and Dr. Cross pulled me aside in the locker room and told me they were naming me head coach."

I said, "Bud, I stand by what I said, but I wish you a lot of luck, and I'll do anything I ever can to help you."

〜〜〜

*When it comes to great college football, **Darrell Royal** is best remembered for his days coaching the University of Texas, one of Oklahoma's two biggest rivals, in the sixties and seventies, leading the Longhorns to three national titles (1963, 1969, 1970). By birthright, however, Royal is a true Oklahoman, who grew up on the plains of the Okie state and later starred under Wilkinson playing for the Sooners:*

University of Oklahoma football was a very big deal. I'm a native Oklahoman, and I grew up during the depression, during the Dust Bowl, during *The Grapes of Wrath*. Just like in the book, my family moved to California in those days looking for work. Those were in the days when mention of the term "Okie" was about like what saying "the n word" is now. Oklahoma didn't have much to be proud of. We had a stigma that had been placed on us with that *Grapes of Wrath* thing.

Two things then happened: the stage play Oklahoma!, which was a big lift for the state's morale; Gordon MacRae. The next thing right along with it was the Oklahoma football program. In fact, Oklahoma! was playing in New York at the same time we went up to play West Point (1946), the first college game in which I played. It was when Doc Blanchard and Glenn David were playing for Army.

Just before that was the depression and we had just had World War II. Oklahoma had been kicked around for a while. At least that was my experience from it.

I personally experienced the "grapes of wrath." After we moved to California, I didn't stay very long. I was fourteen. I hitchhiked back home after about two or three months. I lived with my grandmother when I got back to Oklahoma. I played high school football and went into the service out of high school. Served during World War II, and when we were all

11

discharged, I was contacted by Oklahoma to go play ball there, and that's where I wanted to go. So that's where I went. I wanted to be a coach. And after I graduated from business school, that's what I did—I went straight into coaching.

❧

As for Wilkinson, the way **Pat O'Neal** *remembers it, Wilkinson hadn't been dead set on going into coaching when he arrived in Norman in 1946:*

The funny thing is, he never intended to go into coaching. Tatum talked Bud Wilkinson into going into the job interview with him. They called Tatum and told him he had the job, but with only one condition, that he bring Wilkinson with him. Wilkinson said he would come just for one year to help get things started and that would be it for him.

They didn't have a sizable staff in those days—just three or four assistants and some graduate assistants. Coach Wilkinson was hands-on with the offensive backfield and the quarterbacks. He would draw things on the chalkboard, and when you got out on the field you did things exactly as you were told to. He did things over and over and over again. There were so many people out there on the practice field that you really had to do something special to get someone to watch you. If you knocked the crap out of somebody, you got his attention pretty quick. Oh, he loved hearing a good hit.

❧

Bob Ewbank *played at Oklahoma in 1948 and 1952, with some service time in between—plus one year with the Edmonton Eskimos in the Canadian Football League:*

One of Wilkinson's first coaching staffs at Oklahoma: (left to right) Lou Hemerda, Bud, William "Dutch" Fehring, Walter Hargesheimer, Bill Jennings, Gomer Jones, and Cliff Matthews.

Bud almost got fired his first year at Oklahoma, since he lost to Texas and Texas A&M. Eventually (quarterback) Jack Mitchell had a lot to do with making things click.

Once Bud was given some time to build this thing and to do some recruiting, he was okay. When Jim Tatum and Bud came to Oklahoma, they practically brought the whole naval air station team with them. We had something like six guys who had been All-Big Six in 1945, and none of them could make the team in 1946. Tatum brought in all of these guys and it cost the athletic department some money, and that's what got the athletic director fired. Tatum had to use that money to bring those guys to Norman for three spring-practice sessions.

Wilkinson was a fair guy and after he took over from Tatum, the players pretty much decided, "Okay, enough of this BS. I want to get an education." Nearly everybody was on the GI Bill—they just wanted to get through with it and get out of school. At that time pro football was not that big a deal, and

13

these guys wanted to get their degrees so that they could get out and get to work.

By the time I returned from Korea in 1952, guys on the team were younger. All the older GIs had gone on. Bud hadn't changed in what he did, but he had changed somewhat in how he approached the younger guys who weren't veterans.

∽∞∾

As hard as it is to believe, considering Wilkinson's quick success at Oklahoma, not everyone in the state was satisfied with the Sooners' 7-2-1 season in 1947 that included losses to Texas and TCU and a tie with Kansas. Leave it to radio play-by-play announcer **Curt Gowdy** *to do his part to promote Wilkinson and Sooners football while touring the state:*

I always said I'd rather broadcast a winner than a loser. It's easy to broadcast a winner; everybody is happy and everything is upbeat. So that was good for me. This station I was with, KOMA, a 50,000-watt CBS affiliate, had a manager named Ken Brown, and he later became one of the owners of the Detroit Tigers baseball team. He was an excellent radio man and he was also sports-minded. He sent me out all over the state, which was kind of a pain because it meant a lot of travel going to things like rotary lunches, not only to promote the radio station's broadcast of OU football but the Oklahoma football team itself.

So I was in great touch with people all over Oklahoma, as I would be going out a couple of times a week speaking all over the place. I would take charts with me that explained the Split-T offense and formation, which many people didn't know about. They were one of the few schools using it in those days. Through all this, I was able to get a good feel of how people around Oklahoma were in terms of how they felt about OU football. I used to come back and tell Bud about different things I saw in different towns and what people's reactions had been. Basically, the football program really captivated the state.

It took time to build the program, but after that '48 season when they went to the Sugar Bowl, they were in with the fans. In '49 they were a spectacular team and they were now on their way.

❦

Gowdy, who decades later would achieve national fame as a network television sports commentator, offers this story of how he ended up broadcasting Oklahoma Sooners football, in the process offering a slice of an American sports scene no longer seen:

Ken Brown drove through Cheyenne, Wyoming, one night when I was doing a local high school basketball game. I had gone into the service to be a fighter pilot, but I had a bad back, a ruptured disk in my spine. I went back home to Cheyenne, where the manager of the local radio station called me one day and asked me if I wanted to do a six-man football game between Pine Bluff and Saint Mary's High. I didn't know anything about six-man football—I had never seen a game in my life.

I went out and did the game. The field was nothing but a vacant lot with two soapboxes in the middle with goalposts at each end, and there were no yardage or sideline markings on the field. Plus it was a freezing day. Then when the players ran off of their buses and onto the field, I could see that they had no numbers on their backs.

I made up the whole game, using names of guys I had met in the Air Corps and guys I had played basketball against while in college. That night I get a call from the guy at the station, Bill Grove, and he tells me, "You know, Curt, I'm not much of a sports guy, but you're a natural play-by-play announcer. Do you

Bud's GQ pose, long before there was a GQ.

OKLAHOMA UNIVERSITY FOOTBALL MEDIA RELATIONS OFFICE

want to do high school basketball games this winter?" I said sure, because I had nothing else to do. And that's the only job I've ever had since. Even much later when I would be doing a Super Bowl or whatever, I could still see glimpses in my mind of those two soapboxes sitting out there in the middle of that vacant lot.

Brown drove through town one time and heard me doing a high school basketball game. I guess he was impressed, because he stopped and called the station and asked them who I was, and they told him. He called me about eleven o'clock that night at my house, introduced himself on the phone—I thought it was one of my buddies fooling with me—and I said, "C'mon." And he said, "No, really, I'm going to check into a hotel, and you can call back and verify it. My name is Kenyon Brown, and I'd like you to come down and have breakfast with me in the morning. I want to talk to you."

I went down to meet him the next morning and he explained to me how they had just gotten the rights to University of Oklahoma football. Exclusive rights. He said, "I've got a guy now who is the sports director and he's been giving me a lot of trouble, like drinking too much. Would you be interested in coming to Oklahoma City?" I said, "Hell, yes." That was March. He called me back in June and said he had just let the other guy go, are you ready to come to Oklahoma City. And that's how I got down there.

❧❧❧

Pat O'Neal *didn't get to Oklahoma until 1951, but his assessment of the players' closeness as teammates was the result of groundwork that Wilkinson had started laying in 1947:*

We lived together, we practiced together, we went to class together. There was a real binding effect there, and it didn't matter where you came from; if you were a part of that group, you were a part of that group. Coach Wilkinson always said we had two first teams, although in reality guys who were on that other first team said they would have preferred to be on that first team. It also took a certified public accountant to keep track of who was in the game and who wasn't. It hurt some really fine football players, especially offensively oriented players. If you were a defensive player, it enhanced your position. The way to win ball games was to be as strong defensively as you could possibly be. Build the defense first and then convert defensive players into offensive players.

Oklahoma!

In seventeen seasons as head coach of the Oklahoma Sooners, Wilkinson created and perfected an identity of Sooners football that made it one of the most recognizable programs in the country. Almost every high school football star in Oklahoma wanted to play for Wilkinson, as did hordes of native Texans willing to swim across the Red River if need be to play for the best dog-gone college football program in the nation.

OU football had its various distinctions: deep rosters loaded with lean, white players who were as quick *on* their feet as they were quick *with* their feet; a Split-T offense that could spread the field and open gaping holes for rabbit-like backs to slash through; and a charismatic, soft-spoken head coach with the organizational skills of a corporate CEO, the speaking skills of a seasoned attorney, and the looks of a catalog model. These teams could run and run, and Wilkinson's several platoons of two-way players could wear opponents down while running them off the field.

NCAA rules were lax in those days with little in the way of recruiting restrictions or scholarship limitations. Not that Wilkinson merely had to unlock the gates and wait as dozens of All-Americans-to-be poured through the doors, although that wasn't far from the truth. Wilkinson did recruit and he recruited very well. There's an old saying in college recruiting that says to recruit well, a coach has to recruit the mothers, and no other coach could charm a mom like Wilkinson could. Even if desired players had committed to other schools, Wilkinson could pull them away to Oklahoma with little trouble.

ᏨᎥᎥᎥᎥᏇ

Oklahoma football was a nationally known phenomenon long before **Barry Switzer** *took over the reins in 1973, as Switzer himself attests:*

When I grew up, college football was all about Notre Dame and Oklahoma. I remember having a map that I had gotten from some magazine like *Collier's*. It was a map of the United States, and I posted it on the wall right above my bed. The map showed the mascots of all the well-known schools placed where each school was located. The tradition of the school determined what the size of the mascot was on the map. Oklahoma had the Boomer Sooner and Notre Dame the leprechaun, and those two mascots were much bigger than all the rest. You took one look at the map and your eyes went straight to those two schools because they were the largest on the map. They were the two giants of college football. So I was an Oklahoma fan when I was in high school in the early fifties.

ᏨᎥᎥᎥᎥᏇ

David Baker played quarterback at Oklahoma in the late fifties, by which time Wilkinson's legendary status had taken on a whole new meaning:

Mystique is the right word. He had no Oklahoma background at all. He was kind of a foreigner, so to speak. He kind of landed in our backyard and was the right man at the right time for Oklahoma. That's why people in Oklahoma are so upset with the book that (Jim) Dent wrote (*The Undefeated*, which reported some of Wilkinson's human failings, such as alleged extramarital "activity."). To them, he really abused their hero, and that's impossible for a lot of people to accept. They can't accept the fact that maybe he wasn't as perfect as we thought he was then. I'm not saying those people are wrong or they're right; that's not my position. But that's what is bothering them. Some of my former teammates are really upset.

The way Coach Wilkinson did it in setting his team up was to start by putting together his twenty-two best defensive players. Remember, this was still a time in which you had to be able to play both ways. He would get these twenty-two best defensive players and on offense get them situated in some way. I got to play because I was a pretty good defensive player. His thought was that we wouldn't lose if we had a great defense, although we might have a bunch of 0-0 ties. But we weren't going to lose. That was his philosophy.

As a sophomore, my first year of eligibility, I was one of the twenty-two. On offense I wasn't even a quarterback, where I had played in high school. He put me at left halfback, before he made me a quarterback junior and senior year. The first team (eleven players) would go in and play about eight minutes. Then the second team would go in and play about the next five, and the first team would come back to play the last two or three minutes of the first quarter and be on the field for the start of

21

the second quarter. So if you played on the first twenty-two, you not only saw a lot of action, you were actually considered a starter. That's the way we looked at it.

Most schools didn't have as much depth as we did. Coach Wilkinson told me once that, "If I have eight players playing productively, as seniors, out of each class of forty-five players, I consider that a pretty good recruiting class. Take all the injuries, the academic failures, the mistakes—the players who probably shouldn't have been there in the first place—and if I'm left with at least eight players playing, then that's all I need out of each class." Of course, changes in NCAA rules limiting scholarships changed all that over the years.

We certainly were doing something right; you'd see coaches from all over the country coming by to watch our spring practices.

∽∾

As a young coach in his early thirties, the handsome, boyish-looking Wilkinson could pass for someone ten years younger, as OU All-American halfback-to-be **George Brewer** *found out when he got to Norman in 1946:*

I flew into Oklahoma City, and I was met at the plane by the biggest, best-looking guy I'd ever seen, and he had on a T-shirt that said, "Property of University of Oklahoma Athletic Department." He had a Dodge, which was really rare at the end of the war; very few cars had been built. It turned out it was Jim Tatum's car.

So, we're halfway to Norman and I asked, "What position do you play?" He said, "I'm the backfield coach." He introduced himself as Bud Wilkinson, and I knew zero about OU when I went up there that weekend. I was so embarrassed. I thought, Oh, my God, here I am a crewcut seventeen-year-old trying to

Although it looks like it, Wilkinson isn't really holding his nose. He's focused on Oklahoma Sooners football early in his career at the school.

OKLAHOMA UNIVERSITY FOOTBALL MEDIA RELATIONS OFFICE

play with a bunch of men. I was really embarrassed. He got a kick out of it.[1]

ᘒᙦᙦᘐ

Jerry Cross was one of a number of Oklahoma players who arrived at school in the late forties, left school to spend some time in the service during the Korean War, and then returned to play for Wilkinson. Cross, who lettered in 1953, explains how and why he ended up at Oklahoma:

Now in those days, practically everyone from my hometown went to Oklahoma State, which was then Oklahoma A&M. I got scholarship offers from some other schools like Oklahoma A&M and Arkansas, but I didn't even look at them because I wanted to go to Oklahoma, even though I didn't have a

23

scholarship offer from them yet. The main reason I wanted to go was to play for Bud, even though Oklahoma hadn't yet achieved the greatness it would achieve under him in the coming years. I knew this would be a good chance for me because by 1949 there weren't as many ex-service guys playing football, and more and more they were looking for guys coming straight out of high school. To this day, I don't know why they recruited me, because I wasn't that good.

Back then, they had a tryout at OU and they invited about two hundred people down. Another guy from my hometown and I went down to try out. This was in the spring. We went down there for three days. They put us up and put us in pads and spent those three days looking us over. I was an end and they put me at guard.

Coming from a small school, I was intimidated by the sheer numbers. They had all the guys out there on the fields all at once running all over the place, and I had never seen most of them before. Most of them were from big schools. They didn't have time to interview each of us one on one. But they had a pretty good idea from watching us what we could do. I don't think I even talked to Bud that whole time because he was working with the backs. When it was over and it was time to go home, we still didn't know who was going to get scholarships and who wouldn't. They were going to write us letters to let us know how we did. I found out when an assistant coach came to see me back at home, and he took me downtown for a chicken-fried steak. He said, "Sign this," and shoved a piece of paper at me. And I said, "What's this?" He said, "Don't worry about it. It's a scholarship to go to OU." This was about a month after the tryout.

I think the most important factor in my getting a football scholarship to OU was speed. I wasn't really that fast, but I was on the 440-relay team in high school and we held the state record, so I guess that made a good impression. I was an offensive lineman about 185 pounds blocking guys twenty-five to thirty pounds heavier. Running the Split-T, it wasn't so much a matter of having to hold your blocks that long. You could be smaller and hit a 230-pound man and hold him out just long enough for a back to scamper through the hole. It wasn't like it is today where you have to hold a guy off the passer for four or five seconds.

We didn't pass the ball that much, and our running plays were so quick-hitting that it was more important for our linemen to be fast and quick than big and powerful. All you had to do was fire out, hit, and hold your block for a second or a second and a half, and the back goes through. It was pretty easy, really. No way I could have played in today's game, unless I was a defensive back.

⁂

Cross goes on to talk a bit about playing ball in the service and then what it was like to play for Wilkinson:

I went there my freshman year and then I joined the National Guard. A bunch of us on the team did that so we could go to camp and have a ball and then go to two-a-days. Ten days after that we got mobilized for the Korean War.

We had an excellent football team in the service because we were undefeated for two years. One thing about going back to Oklahoma to resume playing after being in the service is that we service guys kept things in perspective pretty well. We could be in a game that we were leading, 35-0, at the half, and Bud would give this really fired-up speech just to make sure we wouldn't have a letdown in the second half. Us older guys would stay in back and off to the sides as the younger players, now all fired up by Bud, would go charging back by us on their way out of the locker room and back to the field. We stood back and let them go because we didn't want these younger guys hurting anybody as they went blowing back out through the door. Bud was a genius at pumping people up.

⟨∽⟩

Eddie Crowder was one of a number of prominent All-Americans who emerged at Oklahoma under Wilkinson's tutelage, and he would later go on to become a coach himself, spending a number of years as coach at the University of Colorado. Crowder played for the Sooners from 1950 to 1952, and was eventually drafted by the New York Giants:

There was a mystique to Bud. He demonstrated genius in coaching. He had some insights that were different, even inexplicable. Actually, it's hard to go back and try to explain it.

One time, in preparing to play Oklahoma State, he said, "This is a game in which they will think it appropriate to take some risks. (We were favored by, maybe, three touchdowns.) I've seen a defense where someone put ten guys on the line, thinking that there aren't enough guys to block them and that they will be able to stop the running game. You know, I have this feeling they will try that against us." So he put in this one play, which was a little rollout pass that the quarterback could audible at the line if he saw the defense putting the ten guys up front. But it would have to be an audible that wasn't discernible because then they would be likely to jump out of the defense.

What he had the quarterback do was roll out behind the fullback and the lead running back, while the offside running back would step up to block any defender coming from the back side. The tight end on that side would fake a block inside and then run a straight, forty-five-degree angle to the outside to take the pass, knowing that the safety now wouldn't be able to get there in time. Bam, touchdown! First play. We used that two or three more times in the game, and each time it was a touchdown. People accused him of spying on Oklahoma State. That was ridiculous and unnecessary when favored to win by a huge margin. He just had great insights that I never knew of anyone else having.

ᴄᴍᴍᴏ

Sportscaster **Curt Gowdy** *weighs in with some personal insights about Wilkinson, the pressure he faced as head coach at Oklahoma, and how it affected Bud's wife, Mary:*

Bud really didn't have any insecurities, although he was very concerned that first year (1947) as to why he was under such pressure. He would say, "Geez, we tied for the conference championship. Why are people so upset?" I said, "Bud, I don't know. I guess people just want to win here." After they lost to Santa Clara to open the next season (1948), he was really upset. But then they won thirty-one in a row.

His wife, Mary, wouldn't go to games anymore. She used to go to games and she would overhear remarks made in the stands about her husband, and she just couldn't take it. She stayed home and listened to me do the broadcasts. I suppose I helped make it bearable for her, but winning helped a little bit.

I remember we went to the Sugar Bowl that year, in '48, and they had a big luncheon down there. I went with Bud and Mary to the luncheon. Just before it started, Bud came to me and said, "Curt, would you please do Mary a favor and take her back to the hotel? She's all upset." I said, "Sure," so I got a cab and got in the car with Mary to take her back. I asked her what the matter was, and she said, "Oh, it just upsets me so much to see my husband under this kind of pressure." I took her up to the suite, where I left her, and I think she lay down there for the rest of the afternoon. She was bothered by it all, the pressures of it all. She was a wonderful woman, very sensitive.

ᏳᎯᏲ

Darrell Royal, *himself a coach-to-be, assessed Wilkinson's coaching ability and how he handled the pressure of trying to win in his own way:*

His coaching was always encouragement. He would never think about putting his hands on his players' facemasks or stuff like that. His critical opinion of your play was spoken on the depth chart. You didn't have a hard time catching on to what his point was. But he never raised his voice or embarrassed players in front of teammates.

I learned from him that you don't have to explain victory, and you can't explain defeat, so don't make up a lot of excuses when you get defeated, and don't get too chesty when you win. I would see his quotes in the newspaper and was around him a lot when he was being interviewed, because I was involved in some of that, and he was always considerate of the other side regardless of win or lose.

He treated me great. We got along real well. Of course, I was in a lot more sessions with him than the average player because I was a quarterback, and he spent more time with his offensive backs than any other segment of the team. They were basic sessions, easy to understand, fundamental. He had a lot of patience. His philosophy was to make a first down, move the chains, and then try to make another first down. Every now and then you break plays for long gains, but you don't go out expecting or calling plays that would turn into long plays, unless you threw the deep one, which we never did too much.

That's because we were more concerned with making first downs, and if you make enough first downs, after a while the band starts playing and you're kicking an extra point.

∽∞∾

Royal, a quarterback and defensive back, achieved All-American honors in 1949. By the time he left school, the Sooners were twenty-one games deep into what would become the first of two great winning streaks under Wilkinson:

By the time I left there, Oklahoma had had some good teams. They had been to the Sugar Bowl (twice), for one thing. When I left there, we were sitting in the middle of what would be a thirty-one-game win streak. That was a big difference from what had been there when I got there.

I think my having played there for Coach Wilkinson expanded my prospects of becoming a coach a great deal. I never tried to copy him that much because I knew there would come a time in my career when I might be faced with a particular decisive situation, when it would be easy to think, *What would Coach Wilkinson do?* Heck, all I could think about was, *What am I going to do?* I knew I was going to have to make hard decisions, and that's why I never tried to copy a person, even though I used a lot of his ideas. For one thing, I hope I can say that our (Texas's) practices were as well organized and timed out as his were at Oklahoma. Sometimes before a tough game we would have nothing but a practice week of shorts and/or sweatsuits, and they were short and snappy—a lot of meeting time and a lot of film time. One thing for sure: When we went into those major games, we were going to go into them with fresh legs.

∽∞∾

Wilkinson flanked by quarterback Eddie Crowder, who himself would go on to become a college head coach at Colorado.

OKLAHOMA UNIVERSITY FOOTBALL MEDIA RELATIONS OFFICE

Claude Arnold's *association with Oklahoma might have been one of the longest in history. He played freshman football there in 1942, left school to serve several years in the service during World War II, and eventually returned to school, playing his last season there—eight years after his first—in 1950:*

When I came back, OU was running the Split-T. I considered going other places, but my folks and high school coach talked to me about it.

Jack Mitchell was the starting quarterback (when Arnold returned, in 1946) and he could run the ball, where I was more of a passing quarterback. I was kind of out of place and decided I wouldn't play football for the school anymore, so I played intramurals for two years. I made a bit of a reputation and Coach Wilkinson welcomed me back in 1948, when defenses were starting to catch up with the Split-T a little bit. I came back and played behind Jack Mitchell that year, and then the next year Darrell Royal and I competed for the position. He was expected to be the quarterback because he had been there for three or four years, and he was a great all-around player.

⚭

The positioning of players was a full-time job for Wilkinson and his staff. They had dozens upon dozens of warm bodies from which to choose, and then there was the matter of putting the eleven best players on the field, knowing they had to play both offense and defense in those days of playing both ways. Former player **Pat O'Neal** *recalls:*

I had always been a pretty good defensive player, and that was a plus for me. If you played linebacker, you had to play center or fullback on offense. Take Jerry Tubbs—he was an outstanding linebacker. When he was a sophomore, he really wasn't prepared to play offense, but he was such a great linebacker that they knew they had to have him out on the field and that meant having to play fullback on offense. The left cornerback usually played quarterback when he was on offense.

⚭

Eddie Crowder *takes up the subject of positioning players, a subject that different players interpreted differently:*

I don't believe Bud looked at positioning players by placing his best players on defense first and then looking for a way to make them fit on offense. I know some of the players might think that, but he had a marvelous, astute ability to be able to look at people for what they were. If a guy was a very talented offensive player, he thought it also important to introduce that player to defense and to help him grow as a defensive player, too. One of the beauties of Bud's ability was to respect people for where their strengths were, and I don't think he was slanted one way or the other in terms of favoring one side of the ball over the other in terms of placing his players.

I had always been pretty much a quarterback, although I had played defense in high school as well. It was kind of a given that you had to be a defensive player as well as an offensive player, and vice versa. Of course, that was the rule in two-way football. One of the things he illustrated by his approach to football was that if you were an outstanding player, whether on offense or defense, there probably was a suitable place for you on the other side of the ball as well. He optimized everyone's potential by giving them a fair shot to play.

❦

Pat O'Neal *paints a picture of what athletic life was like at Oklahoma and then elaborates on how well Wilkinson interacted with his quarterbacks, starting out with a scouting report of the upcoming opponent:*

Our athletic dorm had been built during the war as a nurses' dormitory and the rooms were really small. The total capacity was only about eighty-five. You did everything together.

On Sunday evening we would receive a scouting report that covered all the facets of the team that we would play the next week. In addition to the scouting reports, each player would get a list of all their assignments and the list might be quite long. The quarterback would get a separate sheet five to ten pages long that told everything about that next opponent that they knew about the opponent from the past, the immediate past, and what they expected in the future. You got all that on

Sunday evenings, to include breaking down all their defenses, and quarterbacks were told what plays to call against each particular defense.

You had to memorize all that, and then on Thursday morning you went into Bud's office and sat down with him. He would take a pad, draw a football field, draw in a spot on the field and then flash pictures from a slide projector up on the screen of all these different defenses—he'd flick it and then it was gone in a second. You had to recognize that defense and then tell him what it was, and then explain what play you would run. You were taught how to read defenses. Actually, you were expected to name two or three plays to run from that spot he had drawn on the pad, and those had to be plays that had better percentages of succeeding against that defense than anything else. He would then move you all over the field and then ask you what play to run from there.

In the game, it was the quarterback on the field calling the play, but, actually, it was Bud picking the play because he had had us memorize all the different plays, defensive formations, and field-position situations so well that it was only a matter of knowing which one of his plays to call.

On Friday night, you were given a final instruction sheet that you took with you to your hotel room to study the night before the game. Sometimes on Saturday morning he would refresh us on something to make sure you knew exactly where you were going and what you were doing. It's mind-boggling to think how much time Coach Wilkinson and his assistants must have spent behind the scenes getting all this stuff ready to give out to the players. We were well prepared.

At the end of the season, we would have a stack of material that had been pertinent during the season, and it was all his doing. He taught at least five quarterbacks every week. I'm sure the coaches had to be working on this stuff and compiling it while on the plane ride home and that they went to their offices as soon as they returned home. By Wednesday night, it was determined that the hay was in the barn, that everything had been compiled and organized to have us prepared with the information we needed to be ready to play our next opponent.

⌒⟫⟫⟫⟫⟨⌒

David Baker *elaborates on the preparation that a quarterback, for good reason, went through with Wilkinson:*

One thing you've got to remember about those days is that you weren't allowed to send in plays: It was against the rules. During this office session in which I sat down with him to go over play-calling scenarios with him, if he disagreed with me on any of the plays I called, he would patiently explain why. We'd do this for about thirty to forty-five minutes, four to five times a week. And he would do this one-on-one with about three different quarterbacks, so you can see that he spent a lot of his time going over all this play-calling with his quarterbacks. Usually, this was during the morning or early afternoon before practice, all week long. By the time we got to the day of the game, we had already done this for quite a while and he had gotten through to us as to why we should call certain plays at certain times.

Play-calling became second nature to us, and what we called was clearly an extension of what Coach Wilkinson would have been doing had he been right there in the huddle with us. He would give you a range of plays to run inside your own twenty, then another set for between the twenty and forty, and different sets on down the field. Inside the opposing team's twenty, what was four-down territory, he gave us a little more liberty to do something, but nothing that you would call risky. We would do this over and over and over. Every so often, even if he didn't agree with you, he might say something like, "Well, I'm not sure that I agree with you, but perhaps there will be something unexpected that happens that will make your call as good as mine." He made me think that I was somewhat his equal. I knew I wasn't, but he made me think I was.

⁂

Joe Rector was one of a large number of Muskogee, Oklahoma, natives who made their way to Norman to play Sooners football for Wilkinson. Rector lettered there in 1956, 1957, and 1958:

Back in those days there wasn't a whole lot of recruiting going on, outside of getting a letter and maybe a visit from one of the assistant coaches, after which we consummated a deal for a scholarship with a handshake. I don't know if I ever signed anything, but my heart was with OU.

I think I had more respect for Bud Wilkinson than anybody I've ever been around in terms of his being a father-in-law type figure. He was a great guy, well organized, way ahead of his time. His teams were always well prepared. Practice was more important than the game. And he was very fortunate to have a lot of good people around him.

David Baker made the statement one time that "You know, I liked ol' Coach Wilkinson: He gets more out of me than I'm capable of giving."

Colorado and Missouri were really the tough teams in what was then called the Big Seven Conference in those days. But not Nebraska—they were kind of the conference doormat in those days, if you can believe that. So really, there wasn't too much competition.

⁂

Rector remembers the innovative and motivational sides of Wilkinson as two factors that meshed well:

One thing Bud did years before I heard of anyone else doing the same thing was scouting his own team to see what kind of tendencies Oklahoma was showing. The graduate assistants would stay up until two or three o'clock in the morning Saturday night going over the film so as to have the scouting report on Bud's desk by ten o'clock Sunday morning. During the game on Saturday he couldn't really tell how much he was passing on third down or what plays were being run from the right hash mark—that kind of stuff.

He would go over and over plays with us all week so that by the time the game rolled around, we didn't have to think. All we had to do was react. We had only about ten to fifteen plays, really, and we could run them with our eyes closed.

In more games than not, I could tell when the whole damn team—the other team—was quitting. Bud would tell us, "Hey, everybody wants to win as much as the other guy on the opening kickoff, but if you get through the first three quarters, our conditioning will win it for us." And you could see opposing teams just flat quit on us in the fourth quarter. Even by the second quarter, you could see guys on the other team moving in slow motion, not hitting as hard with their tackles and not blocking guys like they had been earlier. Bud had us prepared.

Those years at Oklahoma were the best years of my life. I thought I had died and gone to heaven. We even got water breaks in practice, which we hadn't even gotten in high school. After forty-five minutes we would get a water break, then maybe some sliced oranges after thirty minutes. I kept thinking, *Man, this is great.* We were lucky to have had a coach like Bud Wilkinson. Those were great times. The only thing we had to worry about in those days was the 2.2 beer.

∽

Bob Burris was one of three brothers who played for Wilkinson at Oklahoma. When he left school after the 1955 season, the Sooners were thirty games deep into what would eventually become a record forty-seven-game winning streak:

Two things made Coach Wilkinson the great success that he was. One was his knowledge of the Split-T offense and the other his organizational skill. But don't take away anything from his 52 defense. We ran a five-man front, which not a lot of teams were using back then. The defense lets your linebackers work from the inside out, and it seems like we always had great linebackers.

My oldest brother, Buddy, got out of high school in 1941 and went to Tulsa for a year, then he went into the service for three years during World War II. Then he came back to OU in 1946 when Jim Tatum was there and played for three years. I was in junior high school and went to the games, and it was a great experience. I didn't think much then about going to OU until after I got involved in high school football.

Our high school coach at Muskogee, Paul Young, had gone to Oklahoma, so there was a little bit of an influence there. By the time I got to high school, there were already so many guys from Muskogee going to Oklahoma that it just seemed like the thing you were supposed to do. We were just fortunate to have a lot of good athletes, and we did send a fair share to other colleges as well.

I played fullback and halfback. Coach Wilkinson basically coached the offensive backs. He ran most of all those drills himself. I never heard him cuss, but he sure got mad a couple times when we didn't do things the right way, such as the time when he's holding the dummy and I'm supposed to go one way and he goes the other and I run over him.

❦

Burris *vouches for how meticulous Wilkinson was:*

He was very articulate and detail-oriented. "On this play, you step with your right foot first on a six-inch step, and then your left foot, and if you're going to the left you step with your left foot first, a six-inch step, and then your right foot. . . ." He was meticulous about everything, and he drilled, drilled, drilled until everything became automatic with us. If you stopped to think, you're too late.

❦

Burris *described spring practice under Wilkinson:*

We hated spring practice because he would have two teams on the practice field running drills and two other teams down in the stadium scrimmaging. Then they would switch, so that the first two teams were now scrimmaging and the two teams that had just scrimmaged would go straight into drills. You never had time to sit on the sidelines and watch other guys scrimmage. He made sure everybody was doing something all the time. There wasn't a moment wasted. I hated that. Nothing but hit, hit, hit; work, work, work.

At least during the season you knew you would work hard Monday and Tuesday and then slack off a little bit the rest of the week in preparing for the game. For spring practice, I think we had something like a total of thirty practices where today you have something like fifteen spread out over twenty-one days, and even on some of those days you can't have pads on.

I think he worked us so hard during spring practice because that gave him great teaching time for working with the younger

Wilkinson watching a tackling drill in practice. His practices were relatively short and scheduled down to the minute.

players, a luxury he didn't have during the fall when we had to get ready for another game every week. Second, it gave everyone a good chance to really learn what the drills would be during the fall because he did the same exact thing in the fall with the same drills. When the fall season rolled around, he didn't want to have to spend any time teaching new drills: We were expected to already know them so that we could concentrate on other areas that needed to be learned.

We ran a lot of wind sprints. You've got to be able to run to play football, and he emphasized that more than anything. If you could run, he could find a place for you to play.

If you made a mistake out there, it wasn't real bad. If you made two mistakes, it was bad. Three, you're out. You're way down the ladder someplace. They graded us every week, and grades were posted on Monday.

⚬⚬⚬

Part of making the grade while playing for Wilkinson translated to exceptional hustle, something which **Jerry Cross** *grew accustomed to:*

39

One thing you should know about that so-called hurry-up offense we had, in which guys would bounce back up after a tackle and run back to the line of scrimmage to run the next play, was that Bud had nothing to do with getting that started. That was the players. Bud wanted you to hurry, sure, but the idea of running back to the line was the players' idea. They wanted to hurry.

Bud had the type of ballplayers playing for him that wanted to win and were motivated to do what it took to be a cut above their opponents. You can call it hustle, too. Everybody was in shape. Now, there were cigarette machines available and you could smoke if you wanted to, but if you did, your tongue would be hanging out in practice. He didn't pressure you to do this or do that, but you also knew as a player that you didn't want to do anything to embarrass Bud or the university. We had some boys that embarrassed the university, but they left.

❧

Bob Burris:

Bud always insisted that we hurry, hurry, hurry. This was true in practice as well as games. When you got tackled and the play was over, everybody was expected to hurry back to the huddle. I guess you could call it a hurry-up offense. The second time we played Maryland, which was in the 1955 Orange Bowl, we once ran four plays in forty-two seconds. A lot of that had to do with our being in such good shape because we did nothing but run, run, run under Coach Wilkinson. We ran so much in practice: You ran here, you ran there, and then when you got there, you ran some more.

Speed and conditioning were important factors in how good we were as a team, and he really worked us in those areas. Years later I was talking to Bobby Pellegrini, who had played at Maryland, and he told me, "Bob, we weren't even able to call our defenses against you because you guys were always back at the line of scrimmage ready to go before we were set. We had to call time-outs just to regroup." They weren't used to seeing the kind of speed that we had and with which we worked.

◇〜〜〜◇

Jerry Cross:

I've talked to guys who played ball at Oklahoma State, Tulsa, and Arkansas, and I found out that nobody has what we had at OU: We all stayed together over the years and stayed in touch with each other. We go back to reunions and almost everybody who's still alive is at these, and there's a love shared between us that I don't think you'll get anywhere else. And that includes guys who played there at a different time than I did, whether they are several years older or several years younger.

◇〜〜〜◇

Wilkinson for the most part kept players at arm's length, keeping conversation with them to a minimum while delegating most communication responsibilities to his assistants such as Gomer Jones and Pop Ivy. It was a different story with quarterbacks, though, as Wilkinson kept the lines of communication open with his signal callers, pouring everything he knew about running an offense into their heads. **Eddie Crowder:**

He had a belief, very uncommon now, in part because the game and the rules have changed somewhat since then, that the quarterback on the field had a better feel and instincts for the flow of the game and how the defenses were setting up than anybody standing on the sideline or up in the press box did. Therefore, in his mind, the quarterback is the most qualified player to be calling the plays, as long as he was properly prepared.

He spent more time with the quarterbacks than anybody else. In spring practice, for instance, especially when you were a young player, he would hold personal sessions either with one quarterback or, in some cases, two or three at the same time. He would teach all the fundamentals about recognizing defenses, identifying the best ways to attack certain types of defenses, and the probabilities of success for certain offensive plays in certain situations. By the time you had gone through a series of these sessions, to include keeping a notebook that you wrote a lot of stuff in, you just felt so well grounded in the knowledge of football that he had and which had been transmitted to you. You were on the same wavelength with him. You knew what he would want to call when you went into the huddle.

⟨ﷺ⟩

Wilkinson's winning system was built around recruiting character and speed, paying attention to details, and motivating players to do their best by holding depth charts in front of their faces. The result was an incredible dynasty that play-by-play announcer **Curt Gowdy** *gushes over:*

Bud had a program that became unbelievable. In that '48 season, they won out the rest of the way after losing the opener to Santa Clara, including beating Charlie Justice's (North Carolina) team in the Sugar Bowl. Then the season's over, and I get a phone call one night in my apartment. It's Bud calling from Wisconsin.

I said, "What in the heck are you doing up there?"

He said, "I'm up here interviewing for a job."

"Are you crazy?"

"I'd like to talk to you. My plane is due in around eight o'clock. Why don't you meet me and we can talk about it over dinner?"

So I met him out at the airport, drove into town, and had dinner.

I said, "Pardon me, Bud, I don't want to be a smart aleck, but what can you possibly be thinking about?"

"Well, you know, I am sort of Big Ten-oriented."

I said, "You've got the greatest program going here and you have the whole team back next year, with a lot of sophomores."

Bud had been recruiting heavily out of Texas with some help from a guy named Eddie Chiles, who was out of Midland, Texas, and had gone to petroleum school at Oklahoma. Chiles was a big OU fan. He was hiring these kids in the summer and then sending them up to OU—All-American after All-American.

I said, "Bud, you can't leave. This thing is really rolling. This is going to be the best program in America."

"You don't think I should consider it?"

"You lost me. You're out of your head."

And I got up from the table and walked out. But he stayed at Oklahoma, and the team he had the next year, the '49 team, he would claim to be his best team ever. They had one close game, and that was against Santa Clara in Norman (the Sooners won, 28-21, in a late-season game). Played them pretty good. Outside of that, everything else was 39-0, 34-7, those kinds of scores. You know they beat LSU by a big score in the Sugar Bowl (35-0), and they won the national championship.

∽⁂∾

*Gowdy spent about four years in Oklahoma City before moving on to a broadcasting stint with the New York Yankees, but not leaving town until he had forged a good friendship and understanding of Wilkinson and fellow Oklahoma coaching legend Hank Iba, the head hoops coach at Oklahoma A&M (now Oklahoma State). **Gowdy**:*

Bud's teams were small. He liked the whippets, those lean, 220-pound guys who could get off the ball quickly. During spring training, he would line them up and time them, and the fastest guys would play on defense. That's because, he said, if you make a mistake on defense it's a touchdown, but if you're fast you still might be able to get up, recover, and catch the guy. His teams weren't really big, but boy they were quick.

To this day I find it amazing that I had the privilege of being able to work under both Bud Wilkinson and Hank Iba. Hank Iba was like a second father to me. He was different than Bud. Hank used to ask me questions about Bud a lot, and Bud told me that he would love to meet and talk to Hank sometime because he really admired him. They had a mutual admiration society.

～⌒∞∞⌒ᗡ

*One of many Wilkinson players that went on to stardom in the National Football League was linebacker **Jerry Tubbs**, who played for the Dallas Cowboys, among other teams:*

Bud was intelligent and surrounded himself with a group of coaches that were all on the same page. He could recruit well and was able to say the right things to get guys to do what he wanted them to do.

Our third and fourth teams could have started for a lot of schools in the Big Eight. I remember we had forty-three guys on scholarship my freshman year, and a lot of them were good players. He was smart, with a good system. He worked us hard, but he didn't work us long. One reason we were so successful was that we didn't hit in practice during the season. We didn't have any full scrimmages. Oh, we were active and flew around the field, but we didn't have any pads on. In that respect, he was way ahead of everyone. If you didn't do it this way, you would get beat up and the season would wear on you all that much more. You don't see much hitting in practice in the pros. They can't afford it.

Gomer Jones taught the defense. I don't know which side of the ball Bud knew more about, although in those days we played both sides of the ball.

⟡

*Wilkinson and his assistants played a lot of chess with their depth charts, moving players around to get the best fits and the right players in the right places on both sides of the ball. There were times that players involved didn't know what was going on, and a sense of paranoia came over them. **Tubbs**, perhaps one of the greatest linebackers ever to play at Oklahoma, suffered through a case of depth-chart insecurity at one point, as he explains:*

In my sophomore year, they wanted me to play defense but didn't know if I could play fullback or not, and that's where they moved me to on offense. I thought they were trying to get rid of me. I had been second-team center and they moved me to fullback before the Texas game. They wanted me to play fullback so I could be on the field and therefore available to play defense in their two-way system.

Bob Burris was a fullback at the time and a guy by the name of Billy Pricer started that game, but he got hurt during the game pretty early. I went in and had been playing fullback only two weeks, and I hadn't played in the backfield since eighth grade. I played more minutes in that game than I did in any other game in my career. I ended up playing about fifty minutes. Bud had a good feel for knowing where to put people and moving them around.

We were well coached then. When I got to pro ball with the Cardinals, I couldn't believe the difference. At OU, we had been a first-class organization with a lot of discipline and it was an amazingly good program. At Saint Louis, the coaches weren't as sharp and practices weren't as crisp. The managers, the trainers . . . nothing was as good as it had been at Oklahoma. I figured it out after a while that we had been part of a unique situation with Bud. He was so smart. We were so well organized, and I guarantee you we were in shape, too.

Practices were like a machine. They were precise: We had so many minutes doing one thing and then, boom, it was on to another for a specified period of time. All the time, things would be explained in great detail and we would practice it over and over. Bud was usually the man with the whistle and when he blew it, you moved. I don't ever remember him being up in the tower. I knew Bear (Bryant) was big on being up there in the tower.

When they moved me to fullback, Bud coached me directly. He would get right in there with us and show us how to block, that kind of thing. There would be a tackling dummy there and he would run to and throw himself at the dummy showing me exactly how to execute a particular block. He showed all of the intricacies of how to handle the ball, such as taking the hand-off, and how to do various fakes.

⚬⟶⟶⟶⟶⟵⟵⟵⟵⚬

Wilkinson kept practices relatively brief but intense, and he wasn't averse to stopping practice and sending players to the showers for the right reason. **Buddy Leake**, *who played at OU 1951-54, recalls one such incident of a short practice, and it wasn't a reward for hard work:*

On two occasions during the four years I was there, he called us back together just fifteen minutes into practice and said, "You're all are just learning bad habits today, so we're going to go in now and bring it back out tomorrow to try again." One time that happened, I said to Tom Catlin, who was the captain of the team, "Please tell him that we want to do it right, that we don't want to take it in." Tom said, "No, he wants us to go ahead and go, and that's what we're going to do." Most players dread practice, but he worked us in such a way that we wanted to use practice to get it right. You didn't dread his practices, and on top of that he was so clear, so articulate, about what he wanted you to do, that you would say to yourself, "Hey, we know how to do that. Let's just go do it."

❦

High school football players across Oklahoma and much of Texas knew they were in fast company when they were being recruited by Wilkinson, and once they heard from him or one of his assistants, they were hooked. Count **John Reddell**, *who went to high school in Oklahoma City, one of those so charmed:*

Bud and Gomer Jones came up and invited me to dinner with one other guy, Guy Fuller, who was our big center. He didn't have the grades and couldn't go, but they went ahead and took me. It turned out to be a midterm deal, though, because when I got down there, it was discovered that I was one credit short of where I needed to be. They said, "You can stay here and take the course, or you can go back and take it in high school and then come back at midterm." I decided to do the latter because I was kind of lonesome anyway. I took an English course and a shop class, then returned to Oklahoma at midterm. Because it worked out that way, I got to go through spring practice first, then played football the next fall.

○౬౬౬౬౬౦

Reddell, an end, played football at Oklahoma from 1950 to 1952 before embarking on a highly successful forty-year career of coaching high school football in Oklahoma and Texas. Much of what Reddell learned firsthand playing for Wilkinson stuck with him all those years:

Bud used two platoons, two teams of starters, where almost everyone else we played had a first team and used substitutes beyond that. He had enough players that he had two full teams that were just about as good as each other, and evidently that was a big help. He could put in that second group and other teams might think, *Okay, here we go with the backup boys*, and that was a mistake.

His strongest asset was that he studied details, little details that a lot of coaches miss—details such as faking with the ball. Eddie Crowder, who was as good a quarterback as I've ever seen, could fake the ball so well that he could just stand there and people would wonder where the ball went. Bud insisted that things like this be done a certain way.

Now that I look back on things, you can take the option play and see what he was able to do with it. This past year I watched some high school teams play, and I was watching them run an option play, thinking, *That isn't right. They can't do it that way because it won't work.* The secret of running the option was to take one step in one direction, which makes the defensive man take that one step, and while the defensive guy is recovering

There rarely was a reason for Wilkinson to look downcast during his days as Oklahoma coach. On this occasion, in 1953, Oklahoma is trailing Notre Dame in the third quarter.

from that one step, that's when you break the other way. These teams I saw running the option recently would just step off in one direction and try to outrun the defense around the corner, without having ever faked the ball in there. You don't run the option that way, and I know that because of what Bud Wilkinson taught Eddie Crowder—that little extra detail. If Eddie was going to run the option, he would take the snap, make that one step inside to get the defensive end moving inside, then step outside and take off, and he would have it made.

It was kind of like running pass patterns. Back then they were playing the wide-tackle six defense. I wasn't big enough to run over people as a tight end. I'd get up there and there would be a big ol' tackle, who weighed about 220 pounds or better, sitting in there right off my left shoulder, and I weighed about 170. I wasn't going to wipe him out, but I figured out pretty soon, as far as running out there and catching passes, that I would step in there and lean over, looking like I was going to block him. At the same time I could raise up my eyes and look down the field and see the defensive halfback watching me for a key. He would also see that I was blocking the tackle. So here he came, and when he took about three steps forward, I would release and take off and run away from him, and they could get the halfback pass to me. I analyzed that and tried to copy it—the play-action pass was one of the best things I had. One step in the wrong direction was all that you needed when running a pass pattern. It was little things like that that he taught us in learning how to run his offense.

⌒⌒⌒

Don Brown *played at OU at the same time Reddell did, and his story of being recruited by Wilkinson takes a whole different spin—one that left Texas Tech coaches who had been recruiting him in the lurch:*

My story was a funny situation. I played football at Kermit High School in west Texas. We went to the state finals my senior year. I was a center and defensive end, and I also played in the band. French horn.

I had several football scholarship offers as well as a scholarship to Texas Tech to both play in their concert band and on the football team, so my plan was to go to Texas Tech. This was in 1951. I played in an all-star game in Odessa, after which Ed Rolen, an offensive tackle at the time at OU and an Odessa High School graduate, came to me with Bud. They said they wanted to take me to play in the Oil Bowl game (a high school all-star game between Oklahoma and Texas played in Wichita Falls, Texas). I thought, *Shoot, I might as well get a trip out of this*, so I said, "Yeah, I'll go," even though I wasn't playing in the game.

They took me to the Oil Bowl game. The Texas Tech coaches saw me with Bud and Ed Rolen, and one of them stopped me and said, "Listen, you told us that you were coming to Tech, but we can still win without you." I never did actually go to OU to visit, but I went home and told my folks that I was going to go to Oklahoma instead, that I didn't really appreciate the way those Tech coaches had talked to me that day in Wichita Falls when all I was doing was watching the game. I had some relatives in Oklahoma anyway, and that became the first time I ever crossed the Red River. And I made a good decision, because I was fortunate enough to get a chance to play, starting when I was a sophomore.

After that Oil Bowl game was over, Bud and Ed took me to the hotel where they were staying, and Bud said, "Boy, we sure need a lot of centers bad." He was stressing the fact that I would be recruited as a center, and that was fine by me. But when I went to OU, it ended up that I never played a down as a center. I played guard and tackle as a freshman. When I was a sophomore I played defensive end and offensive tackle. I weighed only 184 pounds. As long as you could get the job done, that's all that Bud cared about.

<hr />

Quarterback **Jimmy Harris**, *who played at Oklahoma in the mid-fifties, originally had planned to play ball at Texas A&M. Along came Wilkinson, and there went Harris:*

I was recruited out of Terrell, Texas, after we won the AA state championship. I was a tailback in an offense that used the single wing and the T formation like Duffy Daugherty's old Michigan State teams. It looked a lot like today's shotgun offense, with the ball snapped directly to the tailback. I handled the ball running and throwing. I was recruited by all the major colleges, especially Texas A&M, with whom I signed a letter of intent. Had it not been for the fact that Oklahoma was also recruiting me, I would have never thought about any other place but A&M. However, Coach Wilkinson came in to recruit me after graduation. After having talked with him and visiting the school, I immediately felt there might be possibilities of my wanting to play for him.

So I left my summer job with an A&M alumnus and went to work as a roughneck for an Oklahoma alum for a "big" eighty-seven cents per hour. I guess one of the other reasons that I decided to go to Oklahoma was that Texas A&M did not have co-eds and Oklahoma did. Having seen Oklahoma play on TV only once, I knew I would like the challenge of being a success-ful part of a highly successful program. Once I got there, I found that most of the recruits that had come to Oklahoma also had come from successful, winning high school programs. This tells you something about Coach Wilkinson's strategy. He wanted players who knew how to win and what it felt like to win.

Before I got to Oklahoma, I was not very familiar with Oklahoma's program, other than the fact they were highly suc-cessful. Growing up in Terrell, I was a big SMU fan. The first football heroes I remember were Doak Walker and Kyle Rote of SMU fame. I had known Coach Wilkinson by reputation but had never known that much about him until going to OU.

❧

Wilkinson wasn't as concerned with the size of his linemen as he was with their quickness and agility. **Don Brown** *fit the mold:*

I was five-foot-nine and weighed 184 pounds. During spring prac-tice I'd get down to about 170, but I could move pretty quickly, which made up for my lack of size. Quickness was the most important thing to Bud. I could get downfield pretty quickly and do some downfield blocking. That's why I got to play.

We ran the Split-T formation, and our philosophy was to get up there on the ball, go quickly, and spread the defense. Make a crease for the backs. We didn't throw the ball hardly at all. We ran inside plays, off-tackle, sweeps, and options. One of those companies that make videos made a video out of some films of our games, and it's kind of comical because in putting in music to go with the video, they used the song "The Eyes of Texas." I get a kick out of that.

❧

Brown talks about how film study also played a role in preparing for the next opponent:

On Sunday we would review the films of the game the day before. We did that at Jipson House, the athletic dorm where we lived, which doesn't compare to the athletic dorms of today. We had a big room upstairs where we watched the films, which were on those old eight-millimeter films. Bud was seated up there in back of the room, where now you have private rooms for every different part of the team. We probably had forty or fifty guys that comprised the varsity packed into that one room. We sat on folding chairs and Bud would critique the game film for us, pointing out both the good points and the bad points.

All the coaches did some talking, but Bud did the most. And we got grades on our play, as we had during two-a-days and during our scrimmages. On Mondays they would have our defensive schemes drawn up, and each position would be given a game plan to study the rest of the week. Tuesday and Wednesday were our big workout days for preparing for our opponent.

❧

After retiring from coaching following the 1963 season, Wilkinson embarked on a new life that included becoming a nationally renowned expert on physical fitness. It was a subject the coach had studied while he was at Oklahoma, and at the time it didn't include weight training. **Brown** *explains:*

We didn't lift any weights. I never lifted a weight while I was in college, not even during the off-season or spring practice. Other schools might have been doing that, at least a little bit, but the prevailing wisdom at the time was that all that weightlifting would get you too musclebound. It would slow down your coordination and agility.

They had a fat man's team that had to run if you got too overweight. Fortunately, I never had to worry too much about that. It's unbelievable the kind of weight-training facilities they have these days. As quick as we might have been then, the game was much slower then, and you can see that from watching the films. Of course, we didn't have any black players in those days, either. Sit-ups? Pull-ups? Running the steps? We never did any of that, unless we were told to do so on the practice field because we had done something wrong. But we did run a lot of wind sprints to get into shape, usually at the end of practice.

❦

If Wilkinson was a type A personality, he didn't show it. He was concise in speech, almost soft-spoken. Fire and brimstone was not his style, although he was a master at being able to fire up his teams week to week, as **David Baker** *explains:*

Coach Wilkinson was a marvelous pregame and locker-room speaker. We were young enough to buy into his stories. Were they the difference in how well we played week to week? I don't know. But it was all part of the package that you accepted, and we enjoyed it, and we as teammates already knew we were part of something special by being there. We were the only ones in the country experiencing this with Coach Wilkinson. That made us a unique bunch, and that's what you want to do with your team or group, to make them feel like there is something unique and special about them.

One story he used to tell us was about a wise man, with a bird, and how every Sunday afternoon the people would go up to his house to listen to him dispense his wisdom. One time he put a bird in his hand, closed his hand, and asked the people if the bird was alive or dead. If they said the bird was dead, he would open his hand and the bird would fly away. If they said the bird was alive, he'd crush it, killing it.

So a young man stands up and says, "Is that bird dead or is it alive?" and the old man says, "Only as you will, my son." Coach Wilkinson loved telling that story. He used to tell that story once about every two or three years, and guys who had played at Oklahoma and left would sometimes ask younger players still in school if they had heard the bird story from Bud yet. We loved it. We would have been disappointed if we had gone all the way through school without hearing the bird story at least once.

⚬━━━⚬

Veteran college football commentator **Keith Jackson**:

Bud understood the emotional factor and was willing to deal with it as much as anyone I knew in coaching. And he let his coaches coach. He coached the coaches, and the coaches coached the kids. So when Bud went to say something to the players or to address them in the locker room before the game, the room would be very quiet, because here came God. He was not loud, but he was always organized and he always presented that persona to the assembled lads that held their attention. As a result, when he was done and had told them what they were supposed to do, they believed him. Basically, at that point, all Gomer and the guys had to do was open the door and say, "Go get 'em."

❧

At Oklahoma, practice made perfect, and practices were close to perfect, as **David Baker** *recalls:*

The other thing about Coach Wilkinson is that he was a great organizer. He was a marvelous organizer. The coaches had these little horns at practice and they blew those horns strictly by the schedule. If you didn't have all your reps in at one station by the time the horn blew, that didn't matter. We knew if there was going to be a two-hour practice, it was going to be exactly two hours long. He had it all on a piece of paper, and each coach had a copy. Even back then I had the feeling that was rather unusual, even if it isn't now. It wasn't a frantic two hours; just a well-organized two hours. It flowed well. He was very, very patient with us. You could fumble it or miss a block, which he didn't like, but he never lost his cool.

❧

There were rare occasions when the student would come back to beat the master, as **Baker** *explains:*

Some time after Darrell Royal became coach at Texas, they voted in the two-point play for college football. The funny thing about that was that Coach Royal had been one of those voting it down, but in the first year of the rule he used a two-point play to beat his old mentor Bud and Oklahoma (1958, when Texas won, 15-14).

⟨≈≈≈⟩

Darrell Royal *went to Oklahoma with the intent of becoming a coach himself once his playing days there were finished:*

I didn't make my wanting to be a coach a secret. He knew why I was going to summer school and hanging around over there in the offices talking to the line coaches and looking at film. He had to know, but I don't ever recall his talking to me about that. I let it be known that I was looking to become a coach because I didn't want somebody to be looking for an assistant coach without our coaching staff at least knowing that I wanted to be considered a coaching candidate.

⟨≈≈≈⟩

After becoming head coach at Texas, **Royal** *became an integral part of the lore of the Oklahoma-Texas rivalry from "the other side," yet his bond with Wilkinson never wavered:*

I stayed in touch with him after I left Oklahoma. We got together socially a lot. He was always Coach Wilkinson to me. But when he called he always referred to himself as Bud Wilkinson, not as Coach Wilkinson. And I can understand that because I don't do that either: I don't refer to myself as "Coach Royal," and nowhere in my stationery do you see any reference to "coach" under or before my name. That's something else I learned from him, even though I think that would have come naturally for me anyway. I'm flattered when people call me Coach, but it doesn't define who I am.

*Wilkinson was big into details and structure, but he wasn't a demanding workaholic as assistant coach **Pete Elliott** once explained:*

He made his coaches enjoy being a part of the staff. One of the things he did that was a little different was to meet very early in the morning. The great thing about it was I was one of those who had young kids, so while we got up real early in the morning, when practice was over, we basically would go home, except during double sessions. We had a chance to be with our families, and I appreciated that. There are times when, until your work is done, you have to stay with it. But there are times when you can make the schedule to be with your family.[2]

*During the eleven-year stretch spanning 1948 to 1958, Wilkinson's Oklahoma teams won an incredible 107 games against only eight losses and two ties. His last five years were a sharp drop-off, as seen in a 31-19-1 record that bottomed out with a 3-6-1 season in 1960. **Leon Cross** was a sophomore on that '60 team:*

Maybe it's the old story of the third generation. We won so long and (then) we got people who really didn't want to pay the price. The leadership wasn't there. Everybody was worried about "me" and not the team. Bud was very frustrated with the 1960 team. He would try different things. He called us all a bunch of quitters once. A few choice things like that, trying to motivate this team. The talent was there, but the leadership wasn't. We were probably a 7-3 or 8-2 team that went 3-6-1.[3]

*Before he went to Notre Dame, **Ara Parseghian** coached at Northwestern, where two of his teams were thorns in Wilkinson's side, beating the Sooners in both 1959 and 1960. Nonetheless, Parseghian still tips his cap in deference to the long-term impact Wilkinson had on college football:*

My experience with Bud dates back to when I first started to coach back in 1950. I became the freshman coach at Miami of Ohio and then in 1951 I succeeded Woody Hayes as head coach. That was at a time when Bud Wilkinson was in his heyday, and I can recall getting ahold of many of Bud's films because of his use of the Split-T offense. He ran it with perfection.

We were very much impressed, and what coaches did at the time was look at films of all of college football to see what other schools were doing and to see if anything they did would fit into our own schemes. I remember being so impressed with how Bud's teams could execute that offense, knowing very little at that time that we would be competing against that (after Parseghian took over as Northwestern coach).

❧

*ic **Parseghian** talks about getting Wilkinson to take part in a coaching clinic at Northwestern:*

Before we even played, which was in 1958, I had had Bud come to Northwestern. We had started some coaching clinics in an attempt to encourage local football coaches to come out and get a free clinic during our spring practice. I invited Bud up to speak at our clinic, and I was very impressed. He was such a handsome guy, someone with a lot of class and dignity, and, of course, he was very successful.

I remember having a nice conversation with him about college football, concerning offense and defense, particularly offense, which he was more involved with. Our athletic director, Stu Holcomb, had scheduled us to play Oklahoma for two years. Bud had been getting a lot of static about not playing many schools other than the Big Eight teams, and some of the talk was about why he wasn't playing more of the Big Ten teams. So they finally did schedule a Big Ten team and they got Northwestern, which wasn't exactly the powerhouse of the Big Ten Conference at the time.

We had a home-and-home series. He brought his team to Chicago a couple of days early, and he took the team to the Chez Paree. I found out later they got some food poisoning and that some of their kids didn't play particularly well because of that. Our kids were keyed up to play the ball game. We just did everything right and they didn't. As far as I know, most if not all of their players were able to play, although some of them didn't feel well. But that was information we didn't get until after the ball game. How much the food poisoning affected them, I don't know, but we did manage to overwhelm them (Northwestern won, 45-13). We had one of those days where everything went right. Even in a torrential downpour, we were able to throw the ball around like it was bone dry.

Oklahoma fans were stunned by the fact that we had beaten them. I got a lot of mail from Oklahoma people telling me how their team would get their revenge the next year because we would have to bring our Wildcat team down to Norman to play them. There was a lot of jawing going on between Northwestern alumni and the fans from Oklahoma. I took our team down there the following year, and we won that ball game as well (19-3).

Those two experiences I had coaching against Bud were successful ones. It may have been that his heyday at Oklahoma was past and he didn't have quite the talent at Oklahoma that he

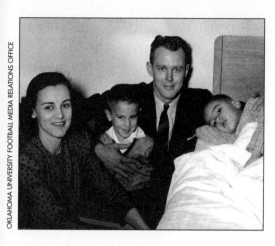

OKLAHOMA UNIVERSITY FOOTBALL MEDIA RELATIONS OFFICE

The original Wilkinson family: Mary, Jay, Bud, and Pat.

had had in the past. On the other side of the coin, maybe some of the other teams were catching up. It's hard to evaluate these things, particularly considering the number of years that have gone by since we played those games.

We were really excited about winning that first game because we had really prepared for it so hard, only for it to be diminished by the postgame comments in regard to the food poisoning. That does kind of blemish it and makes you wonder, "Gee, maybe we didn't beat the team we thought we were going to beat." But the second year when we went on the road and won at Norman, then that certainly was a boost in our hat. It was a little like when we were able to beat Ohio State three out of the last four years that I was there (at Northwestern), with two of those victories coming in Columbus. Those were pluses, no question about it.

ᏅᎢᎤᏊᎧ

Curt Gowdy *recalls Oklahoma's last appearance in a bowl game with Wilkinson as coach, that coming after the 1962 season against*

*Alabama in the Sugar Bowl. It turned out to be an experience bet-
ter left forgotten for Wilkinson not only because the Sooners lost,
but also because of yet another negative experience with a headache
better known as free-spirit player Joe Don Looney:*

Bud had a couple of bad seasons late in his career at Oklahoma,
but then they came back and played Alabama in the Orange
Bowl (after the 1962 season), when Joe Namath was a sophomore for the Crimson Tide. Namath had a good pair of legs
then. I think he gained about ninety-eight yards rushing in that
game—he could run like hell. He had two good knees then.

When I went out to practice the day before the game, Bud
walked me down the field behind the team while they were running some plays. Joe Don Looney was late getting back to the
huddle. Bud muttered under his breath, "I guess his room is out
on the ocean or something. I'm sick of this kid." The thing
about it, Looney was a great punter—he might even have led
the nation in punting. Anyway, Bud was complaining about his
attitude and everything.

Alabama beat Oklahoma, 17-0. Lee Roy Jordan made
twenty-eight tackles in the game and Namath had a big game,
too. That night after the game, I went out to the party they had
at a nearby country club and sat with Bud and Gomer. Bud said,
"You know, I just got outcoached, and they have a better team."
Bud never did alibi. Some guy, one of Bud's assistant coaches,
came up to him and said, "Coach, Joe Don just announced he
won't be back next year." Wilkinson said, "Good. I'm sick of
that stuff. We'll be a better team without him."

Well, Looney did come back the next season, only to punch
and knock down one of the assistant coaches. At that point, the
squad voted to kick Joe Don off the team. It got to be quite a
little scandal down there.

∾

Barry Switzer fondly recalls how, after he had taken over the OU football program in the early seventies, Wilkinson would keep a low profile in Norman so as not to meddle with Switzer's work. Yet, the elder coach would always be there as mentor, if needed:

After games Bud would come by the house with his wife, along with the alumni that came to visit, to have a cocktail with us. I'll never forget that after I took over the head coaching job, Bud told me that he would stay away and not hang around, that he would give me plenty of room to do things, that he didn't want to be seen as a meddler. I understood, just like I don't want to be around (Bob) Stoops or be seen on the Oklahoma sideline. I'm sensitive about that. Bud was that way, too.

So my first year we went undefeated; my second year we went undefeated; and in my third year we finally lost (23-3 to Kansas, ending what had been a thirty-seven-game unbeaten streak). Well, Bud came to my house that night and stayed for two hours. When you win, everybody comes by; but when you lose, people stay away. It really meant a lot to me for Bud to come by and talk to me after the loss. Bud talked about just getting it started again, just like he had done years earlier after seeing his first streak (thirty-one consecutive victories) broken.

31; 47; 94-5-2

Those aren't winning Powerball numbers. They are power football numbers representing the best of the Wilkinson years at Oklahoma:

31: That's for thirty-one victories in a row, a streak that started with the second game of Wilkinson's second season, 1948. It began on October 2, 1948, with a 42-14 victory over Texas A&M following a season-opening 20-17 loss at Santa Clara, and ended on January 1, 1951, with a 13-7 loss to Kentucky in the Sugar Bowl. In between, the Sooners defeated archrival Texas three straight times in Dallas, notched eight shutouts, and won the 1950 national championship.

47: That represents Wilkinson's next big winning streak, which remains a major college football record that to this day has not been seriously threatened. The forty-seven-game streak started on October 10, 1953, with a 19-14 victory over Texas—following a 28-21 loss against Notre Dame and a 7-7 tie at

Pittsburgh—and it ended on November 16, 1957, in a 7-0 loss at Notre Dame. Included in this streak were five straight defeats of Texas, twenty-two shutouts (47 percent of those forty-seven games), and two national championships.

94-5-2: Oklahoma's overall record starting with the first of the thirty-one consecutive victories and ending with that last victory in the forty-seven-game streak, a 39-14 victory at Missouri. That's a winning percentage of .941 over the equivalent of nine-plus seasons. Note: The only conference blemish during that 101-game stretch was a 21-21 tie with Colorado in the 1952 season opener.

Darrell Royal was a part of the Oklahoma program for the first twenty-one victories in the thirty-one-game winning streak:

That could never be done again. Somebody can do something similar, but they can't get there. You put two streaks like the thirty-one-game streak and the forty-seven-game streak together (with a 16-5-2 mark in between), and it's almost like a dream. You're tempted to say, "That can't be."

⟡

*As difficult as it may be to fathom, a number of Oklahoma rooters wanted Wilkinson to be dumped after he kicked off his career with a 7-2-1 record in 1947 that included a three-game stretch of losing to Texas (34-14), tying Kansas (13-13), and losing to TCU (20-7). **Curt Gowdy** remembers those early naysayers and also recalls how Wilkinson got things turned around:*

I was there in '46, '47, '48, and part of '49 before I went up to work for the New York Yankees. In Bud's first year, they won

Oklahoma Sooners head coach Bud Wilkinson.

OKLAHOMA UNIVERSITY FOOTBALL MEDIA RELATIONS OFFICE

seven, lost two, and tied one. They tied for the conference title with Kansas. But a lot of people wanted to fire this guy, thinking he was too young. I think he was thirty-one then. I went around the state defending him, doing these speeches on behalf of the radio station to promote the broadcasts. It got back to Bud that I was sticking up for him, and I guess he appreciated it.

I'll never forget the opening game of the next season,1948, at Kezar Stadium in San Francisco with about six thousand people there to watch Oklahoma play Santa Clara. It might have been the game of the year, even if nobody knew it. Santa Clara would go on to the Orange Bowl that year and Oklahoma would go to the Sugar Bowl.

Oklahoma was leading 17-7 at the half, but blew the lead and blew the game, 20-17. After the game I knew that Bud would be feeling bad, especially in light of all the criticism he had been getting about being too young to be head coach. I went down to where the team was, and they were in this little stucco locker room outside the playing field. You didn't go under the stands to get to them. I found Bud sitting down at the end of a bench, and he had his face in his hands. I could see that he had tears in his eyes. By this time we had become really close, and I went over and put my arm around him. I said, "Geez, that was a tough one." And he said, "Yeah, damn it. We should have beaten them, but they are a damn good team. But, I'll tell you what: We won't lose another game in three years." And Oklahoma went and won thirty-one in a row after that. He could really call the shots.

⚬⚭⚬

Bob Ewbank was a backup quarterback on that 1948 team that opened with the loss to Santa Clara before running the table over the rest of the season to finish 10-1:

I was the number-three quarterback behind Darrell Royal and Claude Arnold. In the first game, Jack Mitchell was at wing-back in our winged T. After the Santa Clara game, we returned to Norman to get ready to play Texas A&M the following Saturday. Bud could not make up his mind about who to start at quarterback. He wanted to make Darrell Royal the quarter-back, but Jack Mitchell had been the quarterback the year before. We had gotten beat at Santa Clara with Mitchell as the wingback.

So we come back to Norman to prepare for Texas A&M the next Saturday. At a team meeting on Monday, Bud said, "We're going to put in some incentives. The incentives are going to be (things) like, if you sack the passer, you'll earn five bucks." Now this was 1948, when five bucks would buy two cases of Bud. "The best faking back will get two bucks. Anyone who tackles a kick-off returner inside the twenty-yard line gets ten bucks." That was pretty big! There were other incentives, too, such as five bucks for an interception. I don't know if it was legal or not to be doing this, but remember, this was 1948, and they (the NCAA) weren't really looking at these things yet.

Now we're playing Texas A&M. They kick off to us, and with Darrell as quarterback, we go nowhere. Although Darrell would go on to become an All-American quarterback in 1949, in 1948 the team just didn't move with him as quarterback. We went something like three downs and kick on the first series and punted, and they (A&M) went down and scored on us. 7-0. They kick off to us, and this time Wilkinson puts Mitchell in. I don't know why he did that, but it was a big splash for us. Jack went left, then right, left, right. In something like four slashes, we were in the end zone.

Here we are now about to kick off, and remember we had this ten-dollar incentive of tackling the kick returner inside the twenty-yard line. We kicked off to Texas A&M, the score 7-7, and you could see from the films where all eleven of our guys were down there inside the twenty-yard line trying to make the tackle. Hey, with ten bucks, one could drink beer for a month! A&M's kick-off team just peeled us away, and Bobby Goode of the Aggies ran it back something like ninety-five yards for a touchdown. But that was the last score they made, and we ended up beating them, 42-14. Mitchell played the rest of the game at quarterback.

☙

Claude Arnold *also was a quarterback during the thirty-one-game streak:*

The winning streak ended when we lost to Kentucky in the Sugar Bowl. That thirty-one games in a row was huge. Other than the forty-seven-game streak that came a few years later, I don't know of anyone else who has even won thirty-one

Wilkinson's foray into network TV broadcasting of college football was a long time in the making, starting in the early fifties when he had his own coach's show at Oklahoma.

straight since. When you talk about Bud Wilkinson and his record over a certain span, with thirty-one in a row one time and forty-seven in a row another time, that's pretty incredible.

The most memorable of those thirty-one consecutive victories was, I think it was against Texas A&M, when we were behind, 28-21, with three minutes to go. We got the ball and took it the length of the field, and Billy Vessels ran a pass in from about thirty or forty yards out to make it 28-27. We missed the extra point, and so we couldn't even think about settling for a tie even if we had wanted to.

We held on defense and got the ball back one more time with about a minute to go on our own thirty. Now, you didn't have two-minute drills in those days. We took the ball down the field and scored with about twenty-five seconds to go. We would never have done that had we made that extra point. I guess you could say that that was one time where missing an extra point actually turned out to be advantageous. People still talk to me about that game, fifty-two years later. Of course, they have to be kind of old to be able to talk to me about it.

Another one was the Kansas game when we were behind, 7-0, at halftime after we had fumbled time and again. To start the second half, they ran the kickoff back for a touchdown and now it was 13-0. But we bounced back and threw four touchdown passes in a little more than a quarter to come back and win (33-13). I threw four touchdowns in another game and ended the season with thirteen touchdown passes, which, believe it or not, somehow remained a record until Cale Gundy did it in the nineties. It's a whole different world now.

⚭

Pat O'Neal *missed by a year being a part of the thirty-one-victory streak, but he managed to stay around long enough after arriving at Oklahoma in 1951 to be a part of the first nineteen victories of the forty-seven-game streak that started early in the 1953 season and lasted seven games deep into the 1957 season:*

If you look at the scores then, you didn't see a lot of really one-sided blowouts, and that's because the play was so defensively oriented. Oh, sure, there were some high-scoring games, but you didn't see a string of a bunch of them in a row. Even during the forty-seven-game winning streak, the scores were held down much of the time, like 13-6 (at North Carolina), 26-14 (Pittsburgh), and 20-0 (Texas) to open the 1955 season.

What happened during this era of dominance was that by the time the second quarter started, most other teams were starting to wear down because their first unit had been on the field almost the entire first quarter, where Oklahoma had switched its first two units to divvy up the minutes. By the time the third and fourth quarters rolled around, Oklahoma was going in with its fourth and fifth units, which were really fresh, and they were blowing by the other guys. For one reason or another, these other teams didn't try to substitute as freely. When you started substituting entire units, you always had to have players out there who were capable of performing every function out there, whether it was offense, defense, or the kicking game.

71

∽❧

Oklahoma's dominance could have been even more pronounced had Wilkinson opted to dig deeper into a playbook that contained some surprises that never had to be used, as **O'Neal** *explains:*

We always had these plays we would run every week in practice but never use in a ball game. Every week we ran these plays, without exception, but we never used them. Then one time against Missouri we scored two touchdowns off two of these plays within a span of twenty-five seconds late in the first half, after we hadn't been moving the ball the entire game. One was a rollout to the right with two wide receivers, for something like twenty-eight yards. They then fumbled the kickoff. We scored on another rollout and we were up, 14-7. We went on to win, 34-13. He always, always had something ready for us to use, but 99 percent of the time he stuck with the usual game plan.

∽❧

Jimmy Harris, *also a former Oklahoma quarterback, takes the ball and runs farther with Wilkinson's ability to keep cards up his sleeve:*

As basic as our offense was, Coach Wilkinson still installed some special plays for us to use in the right situation. In the spring of 1956, knowing we would be playing Notre Dame that fall, Bud inserted some plays that involved putting out a split end and a flanker so as to open up things a bit more, which was something we had never done before. In fact, he created a complete alternate offense that no one else ever knew about, to be used just for the Notre Dame game, and even then that was going to be our fifth game of the season. That's how far in advance he felt comfortable preparing for that one particular game, and also shows to what extent he was willing to go to be ready for Notre Dame, even with four other games to precede it. But then, he had us so unbelievably prepared that off-season—and he knew it—that he could add a few wrinkles into our offense without overloading us mentally.

That (40-0) win over Notre Dame had to be one of the most satisfying wins of his career because it epitomized what a properly prepared team could do against a worthy opponent, even if it was a down year for Notre Dame. Notre Dame is Notre Dame, rain or shine. It could have been a lot worse than 40-0, but we ended up not having to use any of those other plays, such as another one that we called "the swinging gate." The game was on national television, and Bud knew that pulling out all of the stops would have embarrassed Notre Dame. And that is one thing I never knew of him trying to do to any opponent in all his years at Oklahoma.

There were some other special plays Bud installed with us, to include a two-minute drill, that we used very few times. So it's fair to say that there were elements of our offensive attack, as good as it was, that no one other than our coaches and players ever saw. Only a coach as well organized as Bud could have the luxury of adding an alternate offense without taking away from the effectiveness of the base offense, and then be able to win as much as he did without doing anything out of the ordinary.

⌘

Harris saw Wilkinson as a coach whose outwardly laid-back demeanor disguised a burning desire to win, yet it was a steely determination that had compassion as a companion:

Bud wanted perfection out of his players, and he attained it most of the time. He wanted to win, but he never really wanted to lay it on an overmatched opponent either. He told me that I didn't push as hard as I should, that I could be working harder, and I know I should have. In looking back, I can see where I could have pushed more. At the same time, I don't regret it, but I know I could have done better.

One-sided games weren't as common during the dynasty years bookmarked by the streaks of thirty-one and forty-seven consecutive victories as one might believe. While Wilkinson's teams certainly were capable of, as Barry Switzer would later say, hitting opponents for "a half of hundred," it wasn't until 1955—Wilkinson's ninth year as head coach—that one of his teams scored fifty points or more in a game at least three times. **Buddy Leake,** *an Oklahoma player during that era, elaborates:*

He wasn't the type of coach to run up the score on anybody. The Split-T offense was a different mindset, a ball-control type of offense. If we threw seven passes in a game, that was a big day. We didn't have any drop-back passing in our game. We had some in practice, but not in the games. Even if the quarterback dropped back on a play, he might fake a handoff to the fullback on the way. Coach Wilkinson was a real stickler for doing a lot of fakes. I remember being injured and watching a game from the stands one time, and I followed the fullback even though he didn't have the ball on that play. Even I had been fooled, and I knew the plays.

He would always put in a trick play on offense based on how he had seen an opposing defense react in a certain way in a previous game. Like the time we put in a halfback option pass against Pittsburgh. The play was designed such that we threw the ball across the field, against the grain, and it produced a touchdown for us against Pittsburgh. The idea was to keep defenses honest.

A little stretching every now and then while seated at his desk could do wonders for Wilkinson's disposition, which was pretty much even-keeled anyway.

Against Texas A&M in 1951, we had a shotgun offense that we used. I also remember that that was a Saturday night game at College Station, and that was my first road trip. It reminds me of a story, so let me digress a bit. We got complimentary tickets to the game and I remember hearing that we could get twenty bucks apiece for them. One thing about our road games is that we always stayed at a hotel in a nearby city, but not in the actual city in which the game was to be played. On this trip, we stayed in Waco, which is about ninety miles away from College Station. Nobody in Waco was buying tickets, so I asked Billy Vessels if he knew anyone who wanted the tickets and he said, "No, but Coach Wilkinson is always needing more tickets, so why don't you ask him?"

So the next morning after a team meeting, I waited for Coach Wilkinson to come out of the room and I walked up to him and said, "Sir, has anyone asked you for tickets?" and he said, "No, they haven't, Buddy." So I said, "Well, if anybody does, I have three of them that I would like to get rid of." He said okay, and then he walked away. Well, that night, we had a situation where we had like a third-and-four down on their thirty-yard line, and he called me over on the sideline. He said, "If we get a first down on this next play, I want you to go in there and tell Billy (Vessels) to run the shotgun." After the ball was snapped and we ran the play, I didn't wait to see if we had made the first down or not, I just took off to get in there. We didn't make it, so I had to go back to the sideline.

On Monday morning, I get a call from assistant coach Bill Jennings asking me to come to the office. I walk into his office and he told me, "You know, Coach Wilkinson wanted to get you into the game the other night, but he said it didn't appear that you had come ready to play."

And I said, "What are you talking about, Coach?"

"He thought you were too worried about selling those tickets."

"Dang."

John Reddell, *who played end at Oklahoma for three years in the early fifties, was around early enough to be in on the last ten games of the streak of thirty-one:*

I wouldn't say we thought of ourselves as invincible, but we were running along there knocking off everybody by a lot of points. But the conference wasn't very tough at that time. Some of the schools just weren't that good. Oklahoma State had just a bunch of ruffians at that time; they had some coaches that weren't up to par. All they did was come out there and hit you in the back of the head and stuff like that when they had the chance, but they weren't very capable players. Colorado was the big gun, besides us, at that time, and we had a lot of trouble beating them.

Sometimes when things got to where they weren't going very well for us, Coach Wilkinson would make some changes like switching from the option to some other plays. He didn't run many trick plays, but every once in a while he would, and when he did run them they would be quite good. He had a great mind, and I think he had learned a lot at Iowa Pre-Flight. He coached there with Jim Tatum, although he was three times the coach that Tatum was. Tatum was an ol' rough-and-tumble type of guy who never really got the respect of his players and the community, which was something Coach Wilkinson was able to do. Plus we had good assistant coaches with us, like Pop Ivy and Gomer Jones and Bill Jennings. All were good when it came to individual coaching, plus we had lot of players at that time, and it stayed that way for quite a while.

The most important game to me was when we went up to Notre Dame and played, but we lost. We had too many fumbles.

❧❧❧

Jerry Cross *remembers those dominating years as heady times around Oklahoma and in the conference, but there was always the question of how the Sooners really stacked up nationally during an era where national media coverage was nowhere near as prevalent as it is now:*

We looked at how we were ranked in the national polls, but we didn't pay much attention to what was going on around the rest of the country. We expected to be ranked up there and didn't care too much about anyone else. There really was no way to know how Woody Hayes's teams at Ohio State were doing or who was playing quarterback at Alabama because they didn't put any of that stuff in *The Oklahoman*, which was the school paper. We hardly even read newspapers at that. It's not like we felt we were on top of the world; we just knew we were on a good football team.

There were very few people on our team that were cocky. Those that did could back it up, guys like Billy Vessels (who would win the Heisman Trophy in 1952, the only Wilkinson player ever so honored). "Curly" Vessels was good at bragging about what he would do, but then he would go out and do it. It's like Dizzy Dean once said, "It ain't braggin' if you can do it."

Curly and I were freshmen together and ran track against each other in high school, and we got to be real good friends. He was an excellent track man. He would tell you what he was going to do and he would do it. He wanted to win the state championship in the hundred-yard dash. We had two people from my high school in the finals, along with Curly Vessels. Curly came in second and a guy from my high school third, and Curly was beaten by a guy who had never beaten him before. We have a picture from the start of that race which shows that ol' boy who ended up beating them jumping the gun. He was a good two steps ahead of everyone coming out of the blocks. Well, we showed that picture to Curly about two years ago, and he said, "Man, I've always wondered about that. But this proves my point that the guy jumped."

◦⎯⎯⎯◦

Making Oklahoma great was only half the battle. Keeping the Sooners on top week after week was the real test of Wilkinson's coaching abilities. **Jerry Cross:**

He would just keep telling us how we would get beat if we didn't bear down. For example, he would point out how Kansas had gotten beat by Kansas State by thirty-five points or whatever and that we could just as easily lose to Kansas State if we didn't bear down. And he said it in such a sincere, matter-of-fact way that we had to believe him. You believed everything he said.

◦⎯⎯⎯◦

Wilkinson once said the best of his many great teams was his vets-laden 11-0 team of 1949, but an argument could be made for the 1956 team that went 10-0 and scored 466 points while giving up only 51. Almost lost in the middle is the 1952 team that, by Wilkinson-like standards, posted a "mediocre" 8-1-1 record. An opening 21-21 tie at Colorado and a 27-21 loss at Notre Dame, in which the Sooners outplayed the Fighting Irish, were the only blemishes in an otherwise impressive season. That 1952 team featured Heisman Trophy winner Billy Vessels, All-American quarterback **Eddie Crowder**, *thousand-yard-rushing fullback Buck McPhail, and two-time All-American center Tom Catlin. Crowder remembers Wilkinson's astuteness in preparing for particular opponents:*

While we were juniors, in 1951, we played Colorado in Norman. Colorado was a very good team with a collection of really gifted people, like Tommy Brookshier. It was expected to be a nip-and-tuck game down to the wire.

Bud, noticing what kind of defense Colorado played, told all the quarterbacks prior to the game that he really thought they would be especially vulnerable to the play-action pass, such as a counterpass off an off-tackle fake. Their defense was stacked to stop the run and their secondary was so quick to react, that Bud thought they would overcommit too quickly to what started out to look like running plays. Halfway through the second quarter, we were already ahead, 28-0, on four touchdown passes, and we went on to win, 55-14.

The very next year, we were playing Texas in Dallas, and Bud had the quarterbacks come to his hotel room that Saturday morning after he had done everything else to get us prepared. He was kind of packing and getting ready to get on the bus to go to the game at the Cotton Bowl. We quarterbacks went there for what would be only about a ten- to fifteen-minute briefing. I get up there and he said, "I have had a premonition that this

Quarterback Jimmy Harris prepares to take a photo-op snap from Jerry Tubbs, who for a while at least was moved from center to fullback on offense. Harris and Tubbs were two of the mainstays on the Oklahoma team during the latter half of the forty-seven-game winning streak.

game could be almost an exact replica of the Colorado game of a year ago. You know, I just have this feeling that they're going to come up on defense and try to stop Vessels and to stop the option. If we go with the play-action pass early, that will open things up and we can have the same kind of game that we had against Colorado." That was it, and by halftime we were ahead by three or four touchdowns on our way to a 49-20 victory. That gives you an idea of what kind of instincts this man had.

ᏂᎻᎦᎣ

Joe Rector, *who played 1956-58:*

At that time we didn't even know it was a dynasty. Looking back, I can now see where it was a dynasty and know that there's little chance that something like that will happen again, when you have an era that includes both a thirty-one-game winning streak and a forty-seven-game winning streak.

∽∽∽∽∽

Bob Burris, *1953-55:*

The thing about those years is that because we won so much, we tend to remember the games we lost much more than the games we won. We lost one to Notre Dame (28-21) in the first game of the 1953 season, my sophomore year. Then we didn't lose again until we got beat by Notre Dame again (7-0) in 1957, although we tied Pittsburgh the week after we lost that 1953 game to Notre Dame. But after we tied Pitt, we ran off the forty-seven in a row.

∽∽∽∽∽

Rector *remembers the 1956 game at Colorado as the closest call during the forty-seven-game winning streak:*

We were behind, 19-6, at the time. I was third team and that was the only game I didn't get to play in. What I remember is at halftime all the players were sitting around telling each other to "calm down, calm down," but Coach Wilkinson was nowhere in sight. A few minutes went by before Bud pops through the door and says to us, "There's only one guy in the stadium who thinks you can win, and that's me. Let's go play." And we went back there and all the big-name guys like Tommy McDonald and Jerry Tubbs took over, and we came back to win, 27-19. Bud always had the knack for being able to say the right things at the right time. It was amazing, the turnaround.

◦〜〜〜◦

Jerry Tubbs also was around for the 1956 game against Colorado:

I remember at halftime when we were trailing Colorado, he expressed that he still had a lot of belief in us. He was great in preparing us.

One of his favorite stories was the shirtsleeve to shirtsleeve for three generations, about the man who comes into this country and was progressive and tough and built up his business and got well off. Then the son who was there had seen what it took, and he worked hard and built on the business. Then the grandson, he had it made based on his father's and grandfather's work, and therefore he wasn't as motivated and didn't take things seriously enough and ended up in poverty. I bet Bud told that story two or three times during the course of my years there. I bought into it. It was a simplistic story, but it had a lot of validity to it.

◦〜〜〜◦

Tubbs talks about pressure:

The pressure was to win every game each week, not so much the winning streak. That Colorado game at a mile high—I got soooo tired. But here we were, Oklahoma, and we really wanted to win, and I can remember pushing, pushing, pushing to keep myself going during that game. In the huddle we kept saying to each other, "Man, we got to go, we got to go; we got to do it."

I'm not sure that had we not been winning like we had been that I could have motivated myself to play as hard as I did that second half, and I'll bet some of the players felt the same way. So that winning streak did become a motivating factor at times, doing whatever to keep it going and not wanting to lose for the next time. You try to be objective about it, but who wants to be objective.

We had a relatively easy schedule. We played Texas each year and they usually had a good football team, and we played Notre Dame our senior year and they were supposed to be good, even though they won something like only two games that year. But that wasn't our fault. You try never to say never, but I don't think the record will ever be broken for reasons such as the limits on scholarships that tend to balance the playing field. It (the record) sure has lasted a long time, hasn't it?

I can appreciate it now a little better because when you're involved in it you don't see it from the same perspective. Looking back, it sure was good.

ᏬᎥᎥᎥᎩ

*Even during the 94-5-2 era, the Sooners suffered through a slump of sorts. In one stretch, they lost three of four games, starting with a 1950 Sugar Bowl loss to Kentucky and losses to Texas A&M and Texas in the second and third games, respectively, of 1951. **Buddy Leake** recalls some details of that "slump," which ended with a 33-21 victory over Kansas:*

I was a halfback my freshman year. Then Billy Vessels got hurt against Texas in the fourth quarter, and we lost that game, 9-7. The week before we had lost to Texas A&M, 14-7. On the Sunday afternoon after the Texas game, Bud called a team meeting and read us the riot act, saying we are going to be in pads at three o'clock the next afternoon, and the first guy that missed an assignment was going to be out of here. We were getting ready to play Kansas, which was competing with us to be the best team in the conference. That's how I got broken in.

In Bud's pregame talk before the Kansas game, he made several comments about breaking the huddle and say to yourself that you're going to make the best play on that play that you've ever made: "If your assignment is to make a pass, you will make the best pass you've ever made. If your assignment is to run the ball, you will make the best run you've ever made. If your assignment is to make a block, you will make the best block you've ever made." I felt like he was talking directly to me, and I think I scored three touchdowns that day, and it was behind some great blocking. They were leading us in the fourth quarter, but we came back to win, won the rest of our games that year, and won the conference. Everybody had heeded his warning.

Tracking back to the 10-0 1956 team that was ineligible to go to a bowl game because of the conference's no-repeat rule, **David Baker** *remembers:*

The thing I noticed about that 1956 team, in particular, was how the talent gap between us and other teams was just unbelievable. We had so many good players; unbelievable talent. These were guys who could still play in today's game with all its speed. Certainly it was a better team than my junior and senior years (1957 and 1958). We had a lot of guards playing at 190, 195 pounds. We were so quick. I look back now and wonder how we did it, although we didn't see it as a problem back then. We didn't really care. I played defensive back and wasn't that fast—maybe I could've done a 4.7 in the forty—but I was quick and knew how to position myself. I was able to think my way through most situations, but if it ever got down to a footrace, I lost.

All good things must end, and Oklahoma's forty-seven-game win-ning streak was halted in a 7-0 loss at Notre Dame in the eighth game of the 1956 season. **Baker**:

Actually, it took another day or so before it sank into our heads that we had lost the winning streak. For the first few hours after the game, it was just a tough loss against a good team. It didn't really overwhelm us. One funny thing is, it seems like I've met fifty mil-lion people over the years who saw that game, and, of course, we know that can't be true. But that's how big a game it was, how memorable it was. No one ever seems to remember any of the forty-seven games that came before—all Oklahoma victories—but only the one that we finally lost. That's what happens to you.

The game was nationally televised. I can remember how some guy from NBC came down to paint the grass green so it would look good on TV. At that time of year, the grass had turned brown, and that's why they wanted to paint it green. But it rained on Thursday and they couldn't get it painted because of the wet field.

<hr/>

Pat O'Neal reflects on the streak of forty-seven:

As time goes by, it becomes more significant to me all the time. Forty-seven in a row: It's unbelievable, and the fact that I was part if it, even if just for the first nineteen, is really special. Someone had to start it. My brother Jay was there for thirty-one in a row, and my younger brother Benton for twenty-eight straight.

Now, how do you win forty-seven straight games and win only two national championships? You win nine to finish a season 9-1-1, to include beating the national champion in a bowl game (Maryland, in the Orange Bowl). Then you come back the next year and win ten in a row, but you can't return to a bowl game (as conference champion) because you went the year before. And you also have UCLA and Ohio State undefeated for the season, and when you start picking national champions predicated on votes, you've got to ask, where are all the votes? Now we're up to nineteen straight and still without a national championship. The next year we go 10-0 and again beat Maryland in a bowl, and now we win a national championship and the streak is up to thirty. The next year they went 10-0 and couldn't go back to a bowl game, although they won a second national title, and then they win seven straight to start the 1957 season before finally losing to Notre Dame.

⚭

Buddy Leake:

It was being in the right place at the right time with a great group of guys and a great coach. There's a saying that coaching isn't important, it's everything. He believed that every school at our level had, basically, the same level of talent except for the occasional great athlete such as a Billy Vessels here or Johnny Lattner there. But what makes the difference is in being able to put the team together in the correct way, being that it was a team game and such an emotional game.

⚭

*Former Notre Dame coach **Ara Parseghian**, a two-time winner over Oklahoma while at Northwestern in the late fifties, puts the forty-seven-game winning streak into perspective:*

I'd say winning forty-seven games in a row in football is roughly comparable to what UCLA did under John Wooden in winning eighty-eight consecutive games. That's because of the time span involved, where the football streak was accomplished over four-plus seasons and the basketball streak was roughly three seasons. Where I wouldn't be as qualified as someone else in comparing those winning streaks would be in comparing the relative strengths of the conferences in which those two teams played, because so much of each streak had to have involved a large number of games against conference opponents.

⌒⥾⥾⥾⌒

Just for the sake of comparison, **Barry Switzer** *won 87 of his first 101 games at Oklahoma, his best 101-game span, compared to Wilkinson's 94 in that earlier span of 101:*

Bud created a monster, and it was my job to feed it as it was for everyone else who followed him. There's a chapter in my book (*Bootlegger's Son*) about feeding the monster.

⌒⥾⥾⥾⌒

Jim Otis, *a star running back at Ohio State who years later played one season for Bud with the Saint Louis Cardinals, offers this nifty sidebar to Wilkinson's forty-seven-game streak:*

Woody Hayes once went out to see Bud Wilkinson to learn about the Split-T, I think it was, and he met the family as well. Woody had a really good trip. He then came back to Columbus, where he saw his son, Steve, and he was telling Steve about how great a guy Bud Wilkinson was. "By the way," he told Steve, "I met one of Bud's sons, Jay, and Jay got straight A's on his report card." Woody could see right away that he shouldn't have said that to Steve, that he was actually kind of rubbing it into Steve's nose. I think Steve was only about fourteen or fifteen years old at the time. He told his dad how great he thought that was, and then he said to his dad, "You know, Dad, you didn't win forty-seven straight either."

Barry Switzer remembers where he was and what he was doing when he got the news that Oklahoma's forty-seven-game streak had been snapped at Notre Dame:

A lot of people might not remember that I was a college football player myself in the fifties. I was playing for the University of Arkansas during the time of the Oklahoma winning streak. In fact, I was on the team plane traveling from Dallas back to Fayetteville (Arkansas) that fateful afternoon in November of 1957, reading a copy of *Sports Illustrated*, when the pilot came on the public address system and said, "Gentlemen, you might be interested to know about this score: Notre Dame 7, Oklahoma 0." I almost fell out of my chair. Right there on the cover of *Sports Illustrated* was the headline "Why Oklahoma is Unbeatable." I found out that day that no one is really unbeatable.[1]

4

THE GREAT WHITE FATHER

Bud Wilkinson was da man. He was the man in complete control, the man with the plan, a veritable Dapper Dan. His white shirts were impeccably pressed, his tie knotted better than a CPA's, his dimples to die for, his statuesque body a stranger to sweat. He was exceedingly gracious, exceptionally focused, and expertly schooled in all manners of decorum and how-to-score-'em. The only thing out of place was a blond mane quickly turning white, hence the nickname "the Great White Father," a monicker reportedly bestowed on him by player Joe Henderson and perpetuated by hundreds of others.

Players with deadbeat dads, or those without fathers period, who went to Oklahoma quickly found a surrogate dad, or at least a favorite uncle, in Wilkinson. This didn't mean that the Great White Father was a softie given to lots of nurture for his young lads. He was no ogre either. He shot straight with his players, dangled depth charts in front of them to keep them motivated, and carefully chose words that would most effectively stimulate minds, bodies, and first downs. Wilkinson won through intimidation, although he disguised it well.

〜〜〜〜

Jimmy Harris, like others who came before and after him, saw in Wilkinson certain traits that made the coach sort of a surrogate dad:

I grew up poor, and while he personally hadn't recruited me early on, it was easy to figure out that Coach Wilkinson had that knack for being able to look at a person and quickly judge his character. He became such a father figure to me. He was such an impressive person and he had that great winning tradition already firmly established behind him.

My mom was also impressed with him when he came to our house to visit. He was always so neatly dressed, classy, and well organized. My mom had always taught me about being neat and clean. Even if I had only one pair of jeans, I should keep them clean and pressed all the time, and I saw that kind of attitude in Coach Wilkinson.

You had to be mentally tough playing for Bud. That is, you had to be able to think well and process information quickly, and you also had a kind of persevering confidence that would see you through tough stretches in tough games. He wanted his quarterback to be him on the field, and he made it a point to teach you to the point where you knew what to do and how to react in every little situation.

Our offense wasn't complicated, but we went over things over and over and over. The idea was to know the plays so well that, as his quarterback, I knew exactly what play to call in any scenario. His philosophy was that once you called a play in the huddle and the defense didn't look too bad when you came up to the line, then just go ahead and run the play. But if the defense had shifted in such a way to make the called play a no go, I had the option to change the play at the line of scrimmage. The trick was being able to recognize changes in defensive alignments and to quickly surmise what alternate play should be called at the line with an audible. During the week, Coach Wilkinson had the quarterback memorize every contingency and possible defensive alignment so that we would know exactly what to call if I had to audible. The trick was in keeping our offense simple.

As I progressed from sophomore to junior to senior and got more experienced in running the plays, it got to the point that I would change the play at the line of scrimmage about once every seven or eight plays. Still, under Bud, you always felt like you should have already anticipated in the huddle what the right call should be.

‚ûæ

Harris recalls one time that showed just how much influence *Wilkinson had over how he thought and called plays:*

I remember one time playing against Texas when we had a bad snap that led to a loss of fifteen or twenty yards, setting up a second- or third-and-twenty-five. In the huddle I quickly called for a fake punt with a reverse and just then a player that Bud subbed in got to the huddle and said to run a certain play. It was exactly the same one I had just called. That's how well Coach Wilkinson had prepared me.

He worked on an intelligence level that was a little different from other coaches'. In that sense he was a lot like Tom Landry, for whom I would later play when I played for the Cowboys in the sixties. With Bud, it was an intellectual ability to keep your interest, no matter how tedious the practice or chalktalk diagramming plays might be. Other OU quarterbacks under Bud, like Eddie Crowder and Darrell Royal, would get a bigger dose of football knowledge than, say, an offensive lineman would. And when he gave a talk or speech to the players, he had a knack for keeping us on the edge of our seats, spellbinding us, without even raising his voice.

It was the content of what he said and how he said it, that even if you had heard the same message a thousand times, he had a way of making it sound fresh every time. Part of the reason for that was his command of the English language and his ability to analyze things from a variety of angles while explaining it in ways easily understood. Yet he was very patient. He would tell you something once, then twice, and you better have it down by the third time, because there never would be a fourth time. By then, you had been replaced.

Jerry Tubbs, who would play on two national-title teams at Oklahoma, could have gone to almost any school in the nation—Bud Wilkinson saw to it that he didn't go anywhere but to Oklahoma, so powerful was his charisma:

To begin with, his assistant Bill Jennings came to see us at our high school, in Breckenridge. We won a state championship, and we had several guys they were interested in. The main thing I remember is how classy and just how intelligent and smooth-talking he was, and he seemed modest. I was impressed, very much so. They were big winners even at that time, in fall of 1952. A lot of people in town wanted me to stay in Texas, but my high school coach was a University of Oklahoma graduate, although he didn't influence me either way. My mother wanted

Drop and give me twenty!

OKLAHOMA UNIVERSITY FOOTBALL MEDIA RELATIONS OFFICE

me to go to Baylor, because she was Baptist. Some folks in town wanted me to go to Texas A&M or Texas.

Coach Wilkinson carried himself with a lot of class, and he didn't throw out a lot of negative things about other coaches when he was recruiting me. It's not like I was mesmerized by him or anything, but I was impressed. Television then wasn't like it is today, but he was a prominent person, having already won one national championship.

He wasn't the typical college coach. He was no Bear Bryant. On the field, you didn't hear any cursing from him or his assistants—at least I never did. I really appreciated that. Bear Bryant would cuss guys out, berate them, but he was a great psychologist. Bud Wilkinson got the same thing done approaching it from a positive aspect. Players who played for Bear and went through all that probably became more emotionally attached to him, where with Coach Wilkinson, I wouldn't say he was aloof, but there definitely was a feeling of sophistication and intelligence and objectivity, almost as though he were above the fray.

I went on to play in the NFL for the Cardinals one year, ten years with the 49ers, and the last eight with the Cowboys. I was so lucky to be exposed to both Coach Wilkinson and Coach Landry. They were a lot alike in ways. They believed in doing your job, your techniques, the right way every time, and they both expressed themselves well in communicating things to you. Bud was a religious person and I know he went to church, and Tom was such a solid Christian. I don't even know what religion Bud was.

Bob Ewbank recalls how Wilkinson handled a death in "the family":

In 1948 we were getting ready to play Kansas in Lawrence for the Big Six Conference championship. We would always have a defensive meeting on Friday night and an offensive meeting on Saturday morning. We had the defensive meeting as scheduled and then went to a movie in town. The next morning everyone hustled to the 9 A.M. offensive meeting.

At this session Wilkinson calmly said, "Last night I got a phone call from Texas, and (co-captain) Myrle Greathouse's mother died." I still get shaken up when I talk about it. He continued by saying, "I talked to Myrle, and he told me, 'Mom would want me to play.'" There was dead silence. He then said, "The meeting is over. The bus leaves for the game at eleven o'clock." Even the smokers didn't smoke during the bus ride from Kansas City, Missouri, to Lawrence, Kansas.

The game was a massacre. We were up, 60-7, and I ended up playing the whole fourth quarter, offense and defense. For me to play defense was conceding yardage and TDs to our opponent. Coach Wilkinson told me, "Bob, run the ball down the field, pile up yardage, and when you get near the goal line, throw it away." I went into the huddle and told the guys exactly what Coach had told me. Tommy Gray, the left half-back, said, "To hell with that, we're going to score!" Dee Andros, the guard in front of him, said, "Hey, let's call Tommy's play, and he'll score." So, by golly, we did score from about seventy-five yards out. But, alas, the refs called it back because they caught Andros for illegal use of hands! From then on, all we did was run the clock out.

CRILLO

*The powerful Wilkinson influence stayed with his players long after they departed, as **Jimmy Harris** attests:*

I played in the pros for a couple of years and would come back to Oklahoma in the spring to help coach and to finish up work on my degree in geology. I remember going to coaches' meetings, where Bud was so engrossed in what he was talking about and covering all the details. He would bump his knee on something and say, "Excuse me," without missing a beat, thinking he had hit somebody when in fact all he had done was hit his knee on a table or a chair. He would be so focused on what he was saying, and yet he was so polite, too.

Coach Wilkinson was such a big influence on my coming back to school. After I started every game for the L.A. Rams in 1958, they offered me a contract for $9,500, which was less than what I had made the year before. In speaking to Bud about this one time, he suggested to me that I come back to school and finish my geology degree. He said, "When you get to be my age, you'll be glad that you have that degree." He was absolutely right. Here I am now, sixty-seven years old, working at something I really like (as an owner of an oil-and-gas-exploration company in Shreveport, Louisiana). I don't think I would like at this point having been a coach my whole life instead. I can enjoy work without all the pressure.

◎〰〰◎

Harris offers some insights on Cowboys coach Tom Landry, and goes on to compare and contrast him with his college coach, Wilkinson:

Landry, in a way, was cold. Aloof. But then once your playing days were over, he could be your best buddy. With Landry, everything had to be exact. If you were a left halfback, he wanted you in a stance with your left foot forward and right foot back. I said to him, "You know, I'd be more comfortable doing it the other way around." He said, "I don't care. I want you to do it my way."

Early in his career, Landry wore down people in practice, pushing them so hard for so long, and I think he left some victories on the practice field. Bud wasn't like that. Oh, he would work players really hard during the off-season and in two-a-days before the season started. But once the season started, we hardly did any hitting in practice between games. On top of that, our practices were relatively short—intense in terms of how much we covered and went over things, but short enough to where over the long term we were fresh throughout the season. Most of the teams that we beat, we beat in the second and fourth quarters, when conditioning and endurance take over. Everyone was in great shape. Plus, Bud didn't want his players big; he wanted them quick—or quick *and* big.

One way in which Bud was well ahead of his time was in his level of organization. He was incredibly organized and well prepared for everything. Even our two-a-days were structured in great detail, from the time we woke up in the morning until lights out at night, including what we ate for meals and what we were given during practice breaks. I played with four teams in the pros and none of those coaches were as organized as Bud Wilkinson, not even Coach Landry. In an hour-and-a-half practice under Bud, no one ever was standing around. I didn't realize until later how much that helped you get in shape. This was great cardiovascular training even before anyone—other than Bud—knew what that was. I can remember one year when the LSU coach came to watch one of our off-season practices and he couldn't believe it. He had never seen anything like it and couldn't fathom how we were able to be as successful as we were, running nonstop practices like that.

⚬〰〰〰⚬

Buddy Leake:

He didn't raise his voice, even when he was reading us the riot act. There were times that he used a profanity here and there, although even those were words that wouldn't be considered profane by today's standards. One thing I remember that occurred during halftime my freshman year was when Billy Vessels had just scored a touchdown right before the half to make it 7-7 against Texas A&M. Coming into the locker room, having just tied it up against a really tough opponent, we were kind of cheering and hollering. When we got into the locker room, Bud brought us down to earth pretty quickly, telling us that we were getting beat otherwise. That was the only time I ever saw him really get his dander up. One thing he had was dignity.

He always worked with the offensive backfields in practice. The offense was pretty simple, and execution was very important to him. Practice was always very organized, and we were never on the field more than two hours. All the coaches would be carrying around a piece of stationery with the practice schedule typed on it, broken down into how many minutes we would spend doing each drill. At the start, he would bring us all together, tell us what we were going to do for the first drill, break us up into our groups, run the drills, blow a whistle to stop it, and then bring us all back together again. It was all pre-planned.

He was an outstanding person, a very articulate person, although you didn't think in those terms while you were out there on the practice field. He was quite an influence on us. He had his own television program in the early fifties. When we flew to games, he would sit up in a seat right behind the pilots, and would sometimes sit in the copilot's seat, too.

⚬⚭⚭⚬

Leake says if you listened closely to the coach—and who didn't— that over time one could hear things the sounded simple yet turned out to be profound:

Once you had been there two or three years, you started hearing the reruns in terms of him saying the same thing or telling the same stories to make a specific point at just the right time. On Sunday nights, we would have a team meeting and for the first time talk about the opponent for the next week. If we had a weak team coming up, like Kansas State, he would start the meeting off by saying something like, "Okay, men, this week we're going to play Kansas State, and they're going to come at you as hard and as wild and effective as any team we play—for the first five minutes. So you guys need to be prepared to go out there in the first five minutes and show them what you can do.

They don't really believe they can beat you, but you need to go out there in that first five minutes and show them, to prove it to them, that they aren't capable of beating you." Then the next week when we played Kansas, a tougher team, his standard would be the first ten minutes.

❦

John Reddell, like many of his peers, was drawn to Wilkinson as much for his manhood as his coaching ability:

He was a person who had good looks, personality, which was a good start right there. After forty years of coaching high school football myself, I can go back and look and see where he had some really good things going for him.

He was smooth as silk. There was only one time I ever heard him raise his voice to me, and that was when we were having kind of a bad day at practice. I had gone down a couple times to catch passes, and I had dropped two in a row. He said, "Reddell! Come over here! You get over onto the other field until you learn to catch the ball when it's thrown to you."

He crushed me. That put me flat on the ground, so to speak, and he knew it. But here's his way of taking care of things: As soon as practice was over, we were walking into the dressing room. All of a sudden I felt someone walk up from behind me and put his arm around me. It was him, and he said, "You understand what I was talking about, don't you?" I said, "Yes," and he said, "Well, it'll be all right."

That's the way he would keep the respect of his players. He had a great attitude with his players regardless of who they were or how good they were.

❦

Don Brown:

He was a real gentleman coach. He never really raised his voice at all. He did all his damage on paper. We were about five or six deep, and any time you had a bad practice or game, either one, you might find yourself down a few teams. That's the kind of psychology that he used. Players knew they had to perform or they would be spending their time working their way back up the depth chart. You could drop pretty far in a hurry.

When we played TCU one year I didn't have a very good game: I was tripping over the white chalk line a little too much. So I got demoted, and that was the week before we played Texas. I played on the second unit that whole week. Then when we got to Dallas, Bud called out the starting lineup as we left our meetings, and he put me back up where I was.

As it turned out, in the first five minutes of the game, I broke my ankle. Texas was driving and they were on about our five- or six-yard line, and they ran a play off-tackle. I came in a little too high in helping out on the tackle. I got bent back and my feet were in a position where I couldn't move them, and here came the pursuit, and somebody got me on my ankle. It broke a bone and tore ligaments in my ankle. It ended the season for me, which I had hated. I had made some preseason All-American teams and figured if I had a decent season I might make All-American that season. But those things happen.

∽∾∽

J. D. Roberts, another Oklahoma player who would later go into coaching—for a while with the New Orleans Saints—recalled how Wilkinson worked on his behalf in keeping Roberts accountable for his actions after he had been allowed back in school sometime after being forced to leave for an undisclosed reason:

After the meeting with university president Dr. Cross, in which Coach Wilkinson vouched for me and said he would take responsibility for me and my actions, he and I were walking back across campus together. We stopped at the student union. Coach looked at me and said, "Would you like a malt?" I was supposed to be losing weight because I was a few pounds overweight. I didn't know whether to say yes or no. I said, "Coach, I'm trying to watch my weight." And he said, "Oh, c'mon. Do you want a malt?" I said, "Yes, sir." So he got a malt for me and one for him.

We got our malts and were drinking them as we continued walking back across campus to his office. The deal was, I had to report to him weekly to let him know what my activities were and that everything was fine. I would go and see his secretary and tell her that there were no problems, that I was going to class and going to workouts. After about the sixth or seventh time of doing this, he stepped out of his office while I was there giving another report to his secretary. He said, "Jess, you're doing a good job. Just keep your nose clean. You don't need to come back here."

That was the last time I had to go back in there and report, and I promise you that I never got into trouble again. How could I? The next step for me would have been gone, as in not coming back. I kept my nose clean. Being only five-foot-ten and 190 pounds my senior year, I knew I had no future playing professional football, but I also knew then that I wanted to coach, and getting kicked out of school would not have been a good career move for me.

⚬҉ӜҊ҉⚬

Likewise, **John Reddell** *knew while he was still at Oklahoma that his future was in coaching and that he had no one better to learn from than Wilkinson:*

He was so majestic in how he conducted himself. I started capturing and copying everything I could about him, and that's how I got started. I did everything he did, even though I wasn't able to do things quite as good as he did. But that's what I was trying to do. He had such a great way of relating to the players individually as well as collectively. He didn't just get up on a little pedestal. He came over to us and talked with us and sat with us. We really believed in him.

Around that time, while I was in school, my father passed away, and I needed a father figure. There he was. It was Coach Wilkinson. He was a person that I would like to be as a man and as a coach. I wanted to be like him. After I started coaching, I had a chance to go and coach as an assistant under Jack Mitchell at Arkansas. I didn't do it because I didn't want to go all the way out there. Besides, I figured as a high school coach I could always move on to college football later, whereas if I took a college job now and didn't make it at such a young age, then I had flopped.

It was just a great time, the right time for all of this. Going to the Sugar Bowl and all that. I was just walking around with my eyes opened real big, and my mouth open most of the time.

◌◍◌◍◌

Reddell remembers having accessibility to Wilkinson's office, although being there could also take on the feeling of being sent to the principal's office:

You could go over to Coach Wilkinson's office any time. If he could see you, he would invite you to come in, sit down, and talk a bit. If he had something to tell you, or if you weren't doing well, he would call you in.

He called me in one time when I had been loafing or doing something he didn't like. He said, "You know, Johnny, you're doing a really good job for us, but we've got to do something to get you to where you can do this other part," something else he wanted me to do. He said, "You think you can change that?" And I said, "Well, yeah, I think I can." He said, "That's good enough for me. If you tell me that you'll do it, I believe you. I was thinking about dropping you down to a backup unit, but now that you're telling me that you'll take corrective action and do these other things, then I'll start you and play you." Which he did.

That's the kind of way he had to inspire you, and that's the kind of inspiration you could really respond to in a positive way. He could make you think you were motivating yourself without fully realizing that he was the one doing the motivating.

⚯

Reddell amassed a 260-135-12 record in forty years of coaching, the last sixteen as head coach of Trinity High School in Euless, Texas. He didn't win any state championships, although one of his teams that went 12-1-1 was unbeaten (two victories and a tie) against three number-one teams that season in Texas's highest classification of public schools:

After going through all this and going into coaching, I would see times and places where I could use some of the things that he had used. His idea of preparing a practice, for example. Every day when we went out to practice, whether it was to stand around and do some basic drills or going out there to play, the coaches had a typed-out sheet with everything written on there by the minute. Six minutes doing the option to the right, three minutes doing the option to the left, and so on and so forth. It never was, "Hey, let's just jump in there and try this."

The other thing he was real wise in doing was working us on the punting game and other things involved in what is now known as special-teams play, which was something a lot of people were overlooking at that time. We would go out there and run the punt return for thirty to forty-five minutes, doing it over and over. He thought those things were that important, and they were, as it turns out. We'd take a lot of pride in the fact that we were able to return punts as well as we did. We had good return people as well as good punters. We made lots of money off that, too.

I saw what he was trying to do, and it was easy to pick it up. I want to believe that was the reason for the success that I had in coaching.

⌒〰〰〰〰⌒

Ara Parseghian looked up to Wilkinson, even while he was beating the Great White Father:

Bud was the kind of guy that you could look up to. He was a very handsome guy who had been a great player himself. He had a fantastic demeanor about himself, the calmness. He had a very pleasant smile and a pleasing personality. He had every quality that you would want to have in a person that you look up to.

He was a great example for people not only from the standpoint of his being in the coaching profession, but also in how he touched the lives of people in so many other areas. That's why he was successful. If you tried to set the parameters of what you would want the perfect college football coach to be, in terms of what you would want him to look like and think like, and in his ability to communicate with people, then Bud would be the perfect model. Certainly, we, and by "we" I mean our entire staff, in the early fifties already had a great admiration for Bud, not only because of his personality, but also because of his huge success and how well his teams were able to execute what he had set out for them to do.

❧

David Baker, *an Oklahoma quarterback in the late fifties:*

I was not a real fast player. I was a quarterback in high school, at Bartlesville, Oklahoma, which is near Tulsa, and I even ran track because I thought it might help improve my speed a little bit for my senior year. My coach decided it would be nice to have a 100-yard dash competition between his top sprinters while Coach Wilkinson was there on a visit, and I think I came in about fourth. I was so embarrassed, thinking, Well, there goes the scholarship, because the Oklahoma Sooners under Wilkinson were so well known for their speed. But they still gave me a scholarship.

When we heard that he was going to be coming to town, there was a lot of excitement. I had grown up like most other kids worshiping Oklahoma. I can remember them playing Kentucky in one of the Sugar Bowls, and they were losing. I was sitting inside the house listening to it on radio, and I couldn't stand listening to it because they were losing. So I went outside and shot the basketball around for a while. I just couldn't stand to listen to my hero, Coach Wilkinson, getting beat. And Bud Wilkinson sort of played that role as hero at Oklahoma.

Being a quarterback there put me in a position where I was with him a lot more, one-on-one, than the other players were. During the week of a game, especially against someone like Colorado or Notre Dame, I would be in his office at least four or five times just one-on-one. He would have a sheet of paper marked off with a football field, and he would start right off drawing a spot on the field and saying, "Okay, it's first and ten from the twenty," and then it was up to me to call a play. Then he might say, "Okay, you gained four yards with that play on the right side. Now it's second and six; what do you call next?"

The Great White Father didn't yell much, but when he did, there was good reason. Here he's ecstatic during a 34-10 victory over Oklahoma State in 1963, in what would be his last game as Sooners coach.

OKLAHOMA UNIVERSITY FOOTBALL MEDIA RELATIONS OFFICE

This would continue on and on, and we moved all the way down the field.

I know this sounds kind of strange to say this, but he was a beautiful physical man. One thing I can still see is how he had the prettiest fingers you've ever seen, and yet, you wonder, why would I be looking at a man's fingers. Well, he would be constantly drawing on that sheet in front of me as we went over the play-calling. He wore a ring that was quite noticeable, and I couldn't help but find myself looking at his hands all the time. They were just very long and expressive.

∞

Baker also was impressed by Wilkinson's apparent unflappability—well, most of the time:

The one time I can remember him really getting upset was one weekend when a bunch of guys got drunk up in the dormitory and broke up a bunch of furniture, threw the wood in the fireplace, and started a fire. After he heard about that, Coach Wilkinson called a meeting of the football team, and he ripped us up one side and down the other. It was in the off-season and he didn't do anything like suspend players, but he told us to make sure it never happened again, because if it did there would be serious repercussions. And it never did happen again. Oh, sure, there were some guys who did some things that typically happen, but nothing serious.

I don't ever recall his being hostile. Warm and determined, yes. There were times we knew we would be in for a lecture, but never anything that would embarrass us or in which he would lose control. He never embarrassed anybody, at least that I knew of. We held him in such awe, that everything he did was okay by us.

∽∾

Baker admits he wasn't an angel either:

During my senior year, and I won't get into the reason why, I got kicked out of school right before the Orange Bowl. Most coaches in that situation probably would have blown me off and forgotten about me, leaving me alone. Not Coach Wilkinson. He probably spent more time with me then than he had at any other time that I was at Oklahoma.

He sent me to a psychiatrist at no charge to me because he felt I had some problems that would be best handled in that respect, and he wanted this guy to help me out. You would do whatever he said: No one ever refused the Great White Father. I probably wouldn't have thought to do that (see a psychiatrist) myself, but if he thought that was the best thing to do, then I wasn't going to argue about it.

Every so often he would call me to see how I was doing. I know he wasn't a perfect man in all that he did, but for him to take the time and make the effort he did to help me meant a lot to me. He even called my mother to see how she felt about the whole thing, and kept in touch with her after that to keep her apprised of what was going on. I don't think most coaches have the time to do something like that, let alone the inclination to do it. But he did. Somehow he found time to do that for me, and I think he would have made time for anyone else on the team in that same situation.

〇〜〜〇

Pat O'Neal *can still picture the coach on game day, barely a hair out of place:*

He wore a gray hat, red tie, and a gray suit, and he hardly took his jacket off, and then rolled up the bottom of his pants three or four inches to keep the dust from getting on them. Never once did I ever hear him holler to an official to the point of getting belligerent with him.

〇〜〜〇

O'Neal *recalls a sticky moment during the game when Wilkinson tried to give him the benefit of the doubt after O'Neal had made a boneheaded move:*

One time I remember trying for a first down on fourth down against Colorado in 1954, and that was against his rules. It was fourth and four on our own thirty-eight-yard line, and the score was 0-0 in the second quarter. We had been backed up against our own goal line, and it was one of those things where you have a sense of power or whatever, thinking this might be the chance to break something and break the scoreless tie.

I called an option right. They had lined up to receive the punt. We were on the right hash mark. I didn't make the first down, and Colorado went down and scored. When I came off the field, Coach Wilkinson came over to me and said, "Don't you know you're supposed to punt on fourth down?" and I said, "Yes, sir, I made a mistake." He later came over to me and added, "You thought it was third down, right?" I said, "No, sir. I knew exactly what down it was. I just thought I could make it."

There was no way I could have denied it. He didn't say anything more than that, although he had given me an out to defend myself. I could have lied and he wouldn't have known it. My punishment was knowing I had made a dumb mistake. I remember sitting over on the sidelines thinking, Man, you're a senior and you have just played your last game. But our other quarterbacks, Gene Calame and Jimmy Harris, for one reason or another couldn't play, so I went back in. A Tommy McDonald pass to Bob Burris got us down to the one-yard line. Coach Wilkinson had a rule about that situation: The quarterback could call whatever play he wanted, as long as it didn't involve handing the ball off. So I kept it and took it in for the touchdown, and we went on to win, 13-7.

◦〜〜〜◦

Bob Burris:

Bud, like a lot of people, was sometimes a victim of habit. On Friday nights, after dinner, he would typically give a big speech, after which we would go to bed. When we played Texas in Dallas every year, we would stay in a hotel in downtown Fort Worth. During my sophomore year, I sat on the front row as he gave a heckuva speech about playing Texas and about getting rested, and I was just gung ho. I was ready to play right then and it took me a while to get to sleep that night. My junior year, I was sitting about in the middle of the room, and he gave another great speech that got me all fired up, but not quite as much as my sophomore year, and afterwards I went out with some friends to a movie and then came back to the hotel and went to sleep. My senior year, I sat at the back of the room listening to him give the same kind of speech he had given the two years before, and I remember thinking how I wish he would hurry up and finish the speech so I could go do something else.

We stayed in Fort Worth because back in those days they didn't have many big hotels that could accommodate a big football team, and we certainly didn't want to stay in downtown Dallas with all the distracting activities going on around there on the eve of the big game. He wanted to get us away from the crowd and away from the fans, and get us somewhere a lot quieter where we could get some rest. It was really exciting in those days to make that trip from Fort Worth to the Cotton Bowl in Dallas for the game. We had a couple of buses and a police motorcade in front of us leading the way for us over there. That was really neat, and it made us feel really special. They even ran people off the road. In fact, guys were fighting to get on the front rows of the front bus so they could watch all this on the drive over. That was exciting. It was almost like a presidential motorcade.

Texas was our biggest rivalry, so we didn't have to do a whole lot to get ready to play Texas. But we didn't have the media back then like we do now. There were a couple radio stations and a couple newspapers, and that was about it. I don't think we fully realized at the time what we were a part of.

David Baker saw yet another side of Wilkinson, one as servant-leader:

When I was a sophomore in 1956, which was a year in which we won the national championship, we had just played Kansas. We beat them, 34-12, even though we didn't play that well. We were flying back, and I was sitting on an outside seat. This was a flight from Kansas City to Oklahoma City that took quite a while because we were flying on an older plane, and it took a lot longer to fly that route than it does now.

After we had been served our meal and I had eaten it, I can remember turning to look down the aisle to see if it was empty so I could take my tray back to where it was supposed to be turned in. Evidently, when I looked back, Coach Wilkinson saw me and I guess he guessed what I was getting ready to do—to return my tray. He got up from the back of the plane, walked up to me, took my tray, and took it back for me. Now, that might not mean anything to anyone. But there I was, a sophomore on a team with great players like Tommy McDonald and Billy Tubbs, and here's the head coach taking care of my tray for me. That's the kind of man that he was, to me. I remember thinking, My goodness; he did that for me. That was pretty special. He was such a gentleman.

༺∽∽∽༻

*Another thing Wilkinson did for some of his players was to send them up to a summer camp in Minnesota for some leadership experience as counselors, as well as some summertime instruction given by top coaches from across the country who were brought in to lecture. Apparently, NCAA rules about such camps weren't as stringent then as they are now. **Baker**:*

He used to send his quarterbacks up to a camp in Minnesota that he had attended years before while he was growing up. It was a boys camp to which they had added an athletic division. Being a quarterback, I got to go up there for two summers. Bud had come from a fairly well-to-do family, and he had gone to this camp years earlier as just a typical camper. It was a marvelous camp, one of the best camps in America. The DuPont children from Delaware were among those who went there.

Starting in the late forties, they decided to add the sports part to the camp, which was right outside Brainerd, Minnesota. He then had his quarterbacks go there to be counselors doing the same things that other counselors did. Each week they would bring in a different big-name football coach, as well as baseball and basketball coach, to work with these kids ages twelve and up. I'm talking about coaches from places like the University of Iowa and the University of Minnesota—even the coach of the Minneapolis Lakers of the National Basketball Association.

There were two four-week sessions, so as a counselor I got about eight weeks of this stuff. We had kids from all across America coming to this camp. It was a great environment. Counselors, like me, received ample opportunity to be in a leadership role working with these kids while also being exposed to the teachings of all these great coaches that came to the camp. It was an amazing experience. The camp is still there. I took my wife back there about three or four years ago, and it still looked pretty much the same as it had forty years earlier, although they no longer have the athletic camp because that sort of thing has been outlawed (by the NCAA).

⸎

Surviving the rigors of playing football for Wilkinson at Oklahoma sometimes had players thinking of quitting. Some did, but Wilkinson had a knack for talking players out of leaving, even in what seemingly were the worst of times, such as when the heat during Augusta two-a-days climbed well above a hundred. **Baker**:

I remember during my sophomore year during two-a-days when a lot of guys just began to quit. They couldn't handle it anymore. It seems like every day, there were more guys walking off during two-a-days. There was a senior who had played the year before, now a graduate assistant, who came over to the dorm to tell me this story about a guy named B. W.

B. W. was a quarterback, a funny-looking guy who didn't look like a quarterback—a real stumpy guy who was about five-foot-eight and weighed about 210 pounds—but, man, he could throw the football like you wouldn't believe.

My friend came to me this one time and said, "Man, you wouldn't believe what B. W. did."

I said, "What?"

"I was just over at the coaches' office, and when Coach Wilkinson came out of his office, B. W. was standing there and asked, 'Coach, do you have a minute?' Coach Wilkinson really didn't, but he said, 'Well, I guess so.' So B. W. came up and put his arm around Coach Wilkinson (you never touched Coach Wilkinson) and said, 'I'd sure like to talk to you, Coach, and I'll have you know it's not about this quittin' sh—.'"

One thing you never did was curse around Coach Wilkinson because he never did, but my friend told me that Wilkinson about died laughing when he heard B. W. say this, even though B. W. had broken about every rule a player could: taking Coach Wilkinson's time when he didn't have any, touching him, and then cursing in front of him. B. W. was a real character, but Coach Wilkinson didn't recruit a lot of what you called "characters." He recruited character, not characters. To be recruited by him was a great honor, one that I'll never forget. In those days, when you left your hometown to go play at a place like

Oklahoma, you kind of took responsibility for all those people you left behind. It really was a big deal. There was a lot more of that then than I think there is now, maybe some.

❧

Baker:

One thing about him is that he never seemed to sweat, even during two-a-days when it was a hundred degrees out there. I can remember having practice at 6:30 in the morning, and around ten o'clock I would go over to have a meeting with him in the coaches' office. He'd be sitting there looking so neat and cool in his starched white shirt. It looked like he had a personal air conditioner about him. He didn't sweat.

❧

Pat O'Neal:

He was so intellectually advanced, and I don't know how else to say it. And what a figure he cut out on that field, this tall, magnificent-looking man. He was just an icon. We really looked up to him; most of us were in total awe of him.

He smoked cigars in staff meetings. His face was to the chalkboard. We were usually looking at the back of his head.

❧

Eddie Crowder:

As any young person or football fan in Oklahoma, I had heard of him. Everybody thought the world of him, and I was one of those. When I visited the university as a high school senior, I can vividly remember meeting him outside the coaches' offices. My host introduced me to him, and the charm that he exuded was more than anything I had experienced. His aura just filled the whole place. As an eighteen-year-old, it's easy to be very impressionable, but I immediately had this feeling somehow that this man loved me. There was a sincerity and humility about his presence that was so uncommon. It is something I had never experienced before or since.

I didn't feel nervous around him at all. He put people at ease right away, and he did it with humility and sincerity. You were very comfortable around him. He was in no way a guy of pride and ego who would get any sort of satisfaction out of being the eminent person that he was. He not only put people at ease, he made them feel important, and he was like that from the first time I saw him until the last time I saw him.

He had a way of saying the same things over the years without you ever getting sick of hearing it because of how he could say the same thing in a different way each time. He had a unique kind of intelligence, a linguistic aptitude I guess you might say. He had a command of the English language that was Abraham Lincoln-like in the sense that he didn't have to flower up his conversation with words you had never heard before. He could speak in very understandable language, yet he was such a wordsmith that he sounded unique, even refreshing, every time that you heard him.

❦

Crowder would eventually coach at Colorado in the late sixties and early seventies, taking some of Wilkinson's coaching DNA with him:

I'm sure there were similarities between the way he coached and the way that I coached later. One of the things really remarkable about Bud was that he was as well adjusted and stable a person in terms of controlling his emotions and that kind of thing as anyone I've ever been around.

From the first time I met Bud Wilkinson, I've always wondered what it is about him or his background that made him exude such a loving care and concern for people, and that meant being considerate to his adversaries, such as some guys in the press, and he would suffer criticism. But I've read where he was in a train wreck when he was a little kid, real young, and his mother died not long after that for reasons that may have been related to the train wreck. It's said that Bud had this great trauma after the train wreck, and his father literally held him and hugged him and loved him, frequently, almost continually for perhaps a year. That had to be a contributing factor, instilling a lot of personal security in him. A father's nurturing of his son can be such a great expression of love and security, and I think that's what Bud experienced.

~~~

Jerry Cross:

Bud never raised his voice, although he had people working for him who did raise their voice. He had a way of talking to you and instilling confidence that would make you want to run down to the corner store and buy a football magazine to see if you were going to be an All-American. But then you'd go back to practice that same day and return to reality, seeing that you were still on the same team, maybe even second or third string, but you were happy about being there. You're satisfied. I probably talked to Bud twenty times in the time I was at Oklahoma, but it wasn't until after I got out of Oklahoma and came back that Bud and I became friends.

If Wilkinson looks a bit grim, there's good reason. He is standing next to Joe Don Looney, an All-American in the early sixties with a free-spirit streak that tested Wilkinson's patience and authority time and again.

Eddie Crowder *talks about the compassionate side of Wilkinson, which also made him a strong influence as a coach who loved to teach and motivate:*

Speaking from my own experience as a coach at Colorado, in most instances, the toughest players were the sweetest, most humble guys. Hale Irwin, the golfer, was a prime example. (Irwin was a defensive back for Crowder at Colorado.) He's as tough as anyone I know, and look at how he has such a good demeanor. He's a mentally tough person, but he's also a very likable and cheerful guy. He doesn't have the same kind of out-reaching personality as Bud Wilkinson did.

I remember one occasion that involved Ronnie Hartline, who was a fullback at Oklahoma, from Lawton, Oklahoma. He was a very talented guy and might have been the top recruit in the state in his senior year of high school. During spring practice of Ronnie's freshman year, Bud, who was coaching the fullbacks on a blocking drill, was conducting what turned out to be the last drill of the day. Everything was planned down to the minute, and when that last drill was to end, the manager was supposed to blow a horn that would notify all the players spread across three fields that the practice was over. When the horn went off, Bud yelled for everybody to gather around him. This must have been about 120 guys.

Everyone started to encircle him, and as they approached, Bud said, "Stand by, fellows, we're going to do one more block here. Now, Ronnie, let's go block this defensive end," and the defensive end happened to be this big dummy held by another guy. So Hartline goes out and puts his foot down to do a hook block on the defensive end, and the fellow holding the dummy did what he had been instructed beforehand to do—he pulled it away. Hartline fell flat on his face on the ground. There was a little twitter of a chuckle amongst the guys watching this, and here's this poor kid nineteen years old feeling just terrible. Embarrassed. Wilkinson sprints over to where Hartline is lying on the ground. Many coaches in that situation would have said, "You dummy," or something like that. Not Bud. Bud helped him up, hugged him, and said, "Ronnie, Ronnie, you have no idea how close you came to making the perfect block." And there Bud is, still hugging Ronnie as he's saying that. This was done in such a way that fifty years later I can remember it vividly. Those words that Bud spoke are just imprinted on my mind.

He continued speaking to Ronnie, saying, "Let me show you something, Ronnie. All you did was put your outside foot down where it would have been appropriate if the defender wasn't going to move. But by the time that you had recoiled off of that, the defender had moved away; he just got out of your reach. So all you need to do in this situation is put your outside foot down six inches closer to the defender, and then when you recoil you will impact with him. Let's just do one more."

Well, you can just imagine. This time Ronnie Hartline knocks dummy and dummy holder upside down. A great cheer went up from everyone watching.

When Bud said that he developed a killer instinct in people, Hartline was a little bit more of a passive personality. But he developed killer instinct, and Bud developed it in him without brewing animosity in him or by screaming at him. That's astute psychology, and from what I've read, John Wooden, the great UCLA basketball coach, had a similar kind of method of dealing with his players. He loved them and he praised them and he encouraged them, and brilliantly coached them. This is how Coach Wilkinson and Coach Wooden were able to get players who would practically die for them. In Hartline's case, that incident certainly must have made a great impact on him. I was a young graduate assistant coach at the time, and I know it sure impacted me. I can still vividly see the whole scenario.

∽∾

Curt Gowdy:

Bud had a very convincing personality. He could sit and talk to you and persuade you. He was sort of a salesman, a persuader. After all, this was a guy who had a master's degree in English.

∽∾

Darrell Royal offers more details on the influence Wilkinson had in helping to shape his own coaching philosophy:

I always wanted to be a coach. I knew that from grade school. So when I got into organized football and basketball, I always paid attention to my coaches and the way they did things. I was learning something about coaching by being coached in the first place. I did it through high school, through service football, and through college.

Coach Wilkinson had a tremendous influence on me, both as a player and especially as a coach. Until the last day I coached, I was still using some of the ideas and some of the thoughts that Coach Wilkinson taught me. I was never foolish enough to try to act like him or to copy his personality: I grew up in southwest Oklahoma; he grew up in Minnesota. Right there, you've got two pretty different guys. Hell, I was a sophomore in college before I found out I had a "finger." I thought it was a "fay-unger." He wanted to be an English professor more than he wanted to be a football coach—I remember him saying that.

I tried to take what he taught me and use it in my own way in my own presentation and with my own personality. I've seen a lot of coaches ruined by trying to copy some of the personality traits of their coach, and I didn't want to fall into that trap.

‍☕

Royal:

He never really jumped on a player. I agree with Coach that the most important thing a player has is his pride. A coach can destroy pride. The player is in an indefensible position. If he's cursed or yelled at in front of his teammates, he either has to take it or rebel. If he rebels, then he's probably kicked off the squad. Coach always allowed us to keep our pride.[1]

‍☕

Jim Hart was already a seasoned quarterback by the time Wilkinson took over the job as head coach of the Saint Louis Cardinals, and their coach-player relationship lasted less than two years. But in that short time, Hart and Wilkinson struck up what would be an enduring friendship that went beyond football:

Off the field, Bud and I didn't talk football as much as you might think. We talked life. We talked experiences. I mean, here's a guy who had gotten to know presidents and people from all over the world. It really was awesome to sit there and listen to him talk about things. I really liked his low-key mannerisms. When I first met him, it hit me right off the bat that he doesn't fit the mold of coaches like Woody Hayes and others who scream and holler and whatever. I can't imagine anyone not being a friend of Bud Wilkinson's once you met him. What was there not to like about this man?

❧

Keith Jackson:

Bud was very gracious and always willing to let somebody else have center stage—up to a point. He always knew when the time was right for him to step up. As a result, he was able to get young people to play football very well and to do things that they didn't know they could do.

❧

Jim Hart remembers Wilkinson as one cool customer:

Bud was the only head coach I played for who acted on the sideline just like he did at any other time, just like a practice, which was cool and collected. You could talk to him at any time and he was never rattled. He talked to you like it was an office job, even if you came off the field after doing something really stupid.

Joe Gibbs, who was an assistant coach with the Cardinals part of the time I was there, was the same way when he went on to coach the Redskins. Where other coaches might rant and rave at you, Bud would just say something like, "Well, I'll bet you wish you could do that one over again. But you know you're going to get your chance, so get over there and get on the phone with your (position) coach and go get 'em next time."

He just made you feel good; he always made me feel positive about things. He never browbeat me or any of the players. When we started out 0-8 that first year under Bud, there were times at halftime that we should probably have gotten our butts chewed. Yet that wasn't his style. He would talk to us very calmly. The thing is, players get used to being beaten up and whatever, so when he didn't do that, some of the guys would be saying, "Hey, he ought to be beatin' us up. What's the deal here? C'mon." It was all kind of silly, because when they did get a coach who yelled at them, they didn't like that either.

⚬⚬⚬

Andy Sidaris was a director of college football telecasts at ABC Sports for many years, which gave him an inside track on getting to know Wilkinson from all the angles:

Boy, I'll tell you what, he could throw down a cocktail. We'd get on a plane and right off the bat, he would grab a J&B and take a swig right out of the bottle. He wasn't a heavy drinker, but just needed one to settle down after a game because we would have a lot of mad dashes from the stadium to the airport to catch a flight. At the end of the year, we would be doing four or five games in a week with all the bowl games going on. We'd do, say, a Bluebonnet Bowl, a Gator Bowl, a Sugar Bowl, an East-West Shrine Game, and a Senior Bowl in a period of a little over a week, so there were a lot of those mad dashes to catch flights. We were running like crazy. It was pretty hectic but a lot of fun.

⚭

David Baker:

If Wilkinson came to recruit you, that was pretty neat—not just for you, but for the whole community. One time he came up to my hometown and we had a dinner out at the country club. I had never been in a country club, let alone have a dinner at one. With Wilkinson, this was big stuff. He truly was a revered man. Whether he deserved all that, I'm not in a position to tell you. I can only tell you what I saw and experienced.

Bud was a great follower of Ben Hogan. He loved golf and idolized Hogan. He used to tell us about Hogan occasionally. Coach Wilkinson had dinner with Hogan a few times and would tell us how Hogan would sit there with a spoon in his hand, pretending to play every shot he would be playing the next day. This was mental preparation, which is something that Coach Wilkinson used to talk about all the time. He would tell us that even though we weren't playing until that Saturday, he wanted us mentally ready for the game by Tuesday. As players, we could count on well-organized weeks starting with a light practice on Monday, heavy days on Tuesday and Wednesday, Thursday pretty light, and Friday almost nothing.

⚭

Baker describes how Wilkinson's influence over people extended south of the Red River and into Texas, which for decades has remained a fertile ground for Oklahoma football coaches despite the presence of numerous Texas-based Division I schools such as Texas, Texas A&M, and Texas Tech:

Wilkinson recruited north Texas like you wouldn't believe. He just got all the players from Dallas and Fort Worth, Amarillo, Sherman, Breckenridge . . . he just went down and picked who he wanted. In fact, Oklahoma continued to do that for years.

Coach Wilkinson had such a good reputation, and once you go in and have success with one bunch, you had a pipeline established. After a while that began to work against him because his teams got so good, that these players he wanted to recruit started thinking that they weren't good enough to go play for him, and so they would go somewhere else like SMU. I think that started to show up in his last few years coaching at Oklahoma.

಄಄಄

*Wilkinson even held strong sway over Baker's mom, as **Baker** recalls:*

My mother, Edna, was such a fan. Growing up, we would listen to games together. She would occasionally come to Norman to visit me and beg me to take her by Coach Wilkinson's house to show her where he lived. I would just resist with everything I had because I knew, I just knew, that the one time I would go by with her it would be at a time that he was out in the yard or some such and that he would see me and that I would be so embarrassed. So I just wouldn't do it.

Finally, one time, she insisted so much, that I finally caved in and agreed to take her. I drive her over and as we make the curve on his street, we can see him right through a window standing in

Sooners players prepare to get another headful of knowledge from their head coach.

his kitchen, right at the sink, and he looks out and sees us and waves at us. He recognized the car. It wasn't that big a deal, after all, and I quickly realized it had been wrong for me to resist so long taking my mom by. In fact, I came to think that he probably would have loved for us to stop, get out of the car, and drop in for a visit.

ᏮᎭᏯ

Pat O'Neal:

I would hear guys so mad sometimes, upset about something that had happened to them, such as losing ground on the depth chart or whatever, and they would storm out of wherever they were to go over to the coaches' office. It wouldn't be thirty minutes later that they would come back singing "Boomer Sooner." The man was a genius, extremely intelligent.

125

5

THE ABC'S OF LIFE
AFTER FOOTBALL

Wilkinson was only forty-six years old when in January 1964 he announced his retirement as Oklahoma football coach. In one sense, he might have been too young to quit; in another, his resignation might have been overdue. The rest of college football had started to catch up with the Sooners by the late fifties, in large part because new NCAA rules were starting to clamp down on scholarships.

Then, too, perhaps Wilkinson was starting to burn out. Consider this: Between 1947 and 1958, his teams posted an incredible 114-10-3 record. Then came seasons of 7-3, 3-6-1, 5-5, 8-3, and 8-2—adding up to a final five-year composite mark of 31-19-1. That's not shabby, but that's the kind of record that will get you fired these days at Oklahoma, Notre Dame, or Texas.

Besides, there was so much else in life that Wilkinson wanted to do, starting with his 1964 Oklahoma campaign for the U.S. Senate. Wilkinson lost in his only try at elected political office, although by this time he already was befriending

American presidents, hobnobbing with Washington, D.C., insiders, getting involved in the business world, and pushing ahead with a second sidelight career in sports television. It was in television that Wilkinson was introduced to a whole new generation of Americans, baby boomers who were in their infancy while Wilkinson was tending to his dynasty at Oklahoma.

Wilkinson's days as ABC Sports' leading college football analyst, beginning in 1966 and continuing into the seventies, made him a media star as the low-key expert who could dissect X's and O's and detect game trends in a way that informed viewers without overwhelming them. Wilkinson was smooth and an integral cog in the growth of ABC Sports, which brought to sports television a certain pizzazz that went beyond the gaudy yellow blazers.

⚮

*At the same time Wilkinson was running for the U.S. Senate on the Republican ticket in 1964, **Barry Goldwater** was running as the Republican candidate for president. Sentiment among Bud supporters in Oklahoma was that Goldwater's losing campaign against Lyndon Johnson helped drag down Wilkinson's chances along with him. Goldwater:*

It was a big surprise when Bud ran, frankly. The first thing we heard was that he was running. He didn't snoop around and ask questions. He just ran. I like that better than trying to run polls. I spent a lot of money on him. I didn't see how the hell he could ever lose a campaign.[1]

⚮

Dorothy Stanislaus, *a veteran political organizer, was one of those who helped guide Wilkinson's political campaign:*

Some of us tried to convince him not to tie himself too tight to Goldwater. That was strange in view of the fact that I had been a strong Goldwater delegate that year. I had been on the platform committee, and yet I just felt like it was a mistake for Bud to tie in with him. Bud said he wasn't going to upset the ticket. I know the day the campaign kicked off in Oklahoma City . . . right up to the time he made his speech, some of us were trying to convince him not to do it, but he did.[2]

❧

Oklahoma sportswriter **Dick Snider** *was a good friend of Bud's and offered his own take on what transpired on the campaign trail:*

Bud was a great candidate. He worked like hell. Not ever at any time in the campaign did he say, "Aw, the hell with it, I'm going to relax the rest of the day," or "I'm going to take the afternoon off," or "I'm not going to show at that last coffee." Now, he got trapped occasionally spending too much time with people who were already going to vote for him. You had to go to the damn country club or the boardroom at the bank.[3]

❧

Curt Gowdy *offered his take on Bud's failed campaign:*

Bud was very interested in politics. After he ran for the Senate and got beat, he later told me, "Damn, I should have won. I should have worn an old pair of suspenders or chewed tobacco." That's because the guy who beat him (Democrat Fred Harris) was that kind of a guy. Bud would have been the ideal guy for senator, just on his intelligence. He had it all: the looks, the speaking ability, everything.

☙❧

Despite losing the 1964 senatorial race, Wilkinson remained active in the national political scene, in the process forging friendships with the conservative likes of Richard Nixon. During Nixon's second presidential bid, which resulted in a 1968 victory over Democrat Hubert Humphrey, Wilkinson got involved as moderator for Man in the Arena telecasts starring Nixon. **Roger Ailes**, *media adviser to President Richard Nixon, explains Wilkinson's role:*

Nixon trusted him. He admired him and liked him and, most of all, he trusted him. He knew he was stable and wasn't going to do anything crazy. Bud handled the introduction of the panelists and (when questioning began) he would sort of watch Nixon and try to figure out when it was time to move on. He was more of a safety valve once the show started.[4]

☙❧

Lee Allen Smith *was one of Wilkinson's many Oklahoma friends whose association with the Great White Father was not based on football. Smith was, and remains, one of Oklahoma City's most prominent media veterans, a former television executive who for the last fifteen years has worked in advertising. Smith touches on the 1964 senatorial campaign, and more:*

I helped a little bit during the senatorial race in 1964. I contributed a little financial support and put out some yard signs. I wish I had done more. Bud had the unfortunate plight of having to deal with the problem of how Barry Goldwater, the Republican presidential candidate, was perceived by people. In any other year, Bud would have won the race. He did okay, but he didn't know the territory; he really didn't know how to campaign to win. I don't know if he got enough support from the real, true friends that he had. He didn't win the support of some of his players because he didn't make the effort to go out and seek it.

CRMLO

One of **Smith***'s many projects over the years was his production of* The Stars and Stripes Show, *with guests that featured the likes of Bob Hope. Wilkinson was there to help, and oftentimes the favors were reciprocated:*

Bud was always helpful in getting well-known people to come in for the show.

Bud came to me and asked me if I would put together a golf tournament for the Society to Prevent Blindness. Bud and Barry (Switzer) did that tournament in later years. Although I planned it and put it on, to include scheduling all the events surrounding it, Bud was always good about making sure that he brought in people like quarterback Jim Hart from the Saint Louis Cardinals.

CRMLO

By the time Wilkinson did his first bit of TV college football commentary, starting with NBC's coverage of the 1965 Orange Bowl, he already had plenty of TV experience under his belt. He had his own coach's show at Oklahoma on the air by the early fifties and within a few years was hosting the nationally syndicated Sports for the Family, *which was telecast live on Sunday afternoons.* **Howard Neumann** *was co-originator of the* Sports for the Family *show:*

We would meet every Thursday. Bud always said he wasn't superstitious. He didn't believe in stepping on the sideline, of course, and he always wore the same suit and hat to games. But I didn't challenge him on it. So every Thursday noon we met at the same restaurant—a barbecue over on old Route 77. We'd meet on Thursday, because by Thursday, everything was done as far as the game was concerned except his meeting with the quarterbacks. Now, no superstition here, but we would always have the same thing: barbecued beef and a big hot fudge sundae and coffee. Every week, there was no looking at the menu. No alteration. That was it.[5]

⚬⟋⟍⟍⟍⟍⟍⟍⟍⟍⟍⟍⟍⟍⟍⟍⟍⟍⟍⟍⟍⟍⟍⟍⟍⟍⟍⟍⟍⟍⟍⟍⟍⟍⟍⟍⟍⟍9

Wilkinson spent his first year, 1965, in network-televised college football with NBC before switching over to ABC after the latter network reacquired rights to college football. **Andy Sidaris** *was ABC's director for college football telecasts, a role he would fill through 1987:*

Bud came on in 1966. At that time it was Chris Schenkel, and for a minute there we tried Duffy Daugherty as color analyst. We had three of them in there for a while, but it got to be too crowded because college football moves a lot faster than pro football. There's not enough room or time between plays for three guys.

Bud was fabulous. When you hit town with a Bud Wilkinson, and later on an Ara Parseghian—people who are more than coaches; they're legends—you're given every accommodation that the city and college can give you because these fellows meant so much. Bud wasn't so much an X's-and-O's guy and he wasn't overbearing, but he was knowledgeable. He pointed out a lot of stuff, although we were always trying to get him to be more controversial than he was.

Chuck Howard was the producer and I was the director. What we had was a great package with Bud and Chris, and eventually we brought in Keith Jackson.

Bud would party with us all night. Don't kid yourself: Bud was a party animal. He would have a cocktail or two with you and have some laughs. One of the nice things about Bud was that he was such a rah-rah kind of college guy in the greatest sense of the word. He knew every word to every college fight song. We would go to Nebraska or Colorado or Texas and head out the night before to a bar or a really nice restaurant, and he would be singing at the piano until God knows when. He would be leading the songs with such enthusiasm. I'm surprised he wasn't wearing one of those long raccoon coats all the time and carrying a pennant in one hand. He was such a great legend and a happy, smiling guy. He made everybody on the crew feel good. He was polite to everybody; people just admired him, and the humility he had was such a beautiful thing to see.

The guy that worked harder than anybody on pulling the whole telecast together was Chuck Howard. Chuck was a very loud, screaming kind of producer, where I was the kind of guy who never raised his voice. He worked very closely with Bud to make him a better announcer, a more controversial announcer.

ᏬᎷᎬᏬ

Sidaris offers more detail on what it was like to work with
Wilkinson while ABC was emerging as the most dynamic and
innovative entity ever to televise college football:

Working together was classically fun. Bud would get there on a Wednesday or Thursday and meet with the coaches and learn the game plan.

One Thursday when we were out at Southern Cal, and we were out on the middle of the field at the coliseum with USC coach John McKay. The players usually would practice at a practice field until Friday, but they were coming out to the coliseum a day earlier to have some photos taken and to do some interviews with us.

The players come jogging out onto the field to do some laps before practice started, and there's Bud Wilkinson out in the middle of the field. When the players came out, Bud turned around and saw them, and his mouth fell almost all the way to his chest. In comes the USC team, ranked number one in the country, and here's John McKay's team loaded with players who were so much bigger, stronger, and even more beautiful than anything he had seen before. They ran out a hundred guys who were six-five and almost three hundred pounds—like they came out of a cookie cutter, albeit with different colors, some white and blond hair and others black. They were even bigger than the Los Angeles Rams at that time. By comparison, at Oklahoma, Bud would be lucky just to have one two-hundred-pound tackle. Then he sees these guys, 270, 280 pounds with twenty-eight-inch waists. Bud just started laughing, saying, "I've never seen anything like this." McKay sees this and starts ragging on Bud big time, saying, "You should have come to California (while coaching at Oklahoma) to get our guys." Bud was in awe of that.

✺

Sidaris *talks about one of the best games that ABC was ever involved in—a touch-football match at Yankee Stadium that gave the likes of Wilkinson and Frank Gifford the chance to stretch their legs a bit:*

We played it at Yankee Stadium. It was the NCAA guys, such as me, Chuck Howard, Terry Jastrow, and Bud—we called ourselves the Gamecocks—against the *Monday Night Football* crew, with Frank Gifford, Bobby Goodrich, who had been an end at

SMU, and Chet Forte. (Don) Meredith was there, but he coached from the sidelines because his knees were too messed up for him to be able to play. It was a magnificent day and we had people such as Ethel Kennedy out there watching us. I think it was the most fun we had ever had in a single day in our lives.

There were something like eight guys on each team. They beat us, 21-18, because we didn't have anybody who could kick extra points. But I did score two touchdowns. One of them was on about a forty-yard run. The other came when I flipped a lateral out to Bud on the right side and then took off down the field toward the end, with Gifford running with me step for step. Suddenly, I pulled up and said, "Oh, damn, I think I broke my ankle." Gifford stops and then I took off again, and Bud hit me with a perfect bullet that I caught right on the hip for the second touchdown. I looked at Frank and said, "You stupid (jerk). Look at me, dude, I'm two yards into the end zone and you're looking for someone to help me out."

It was just one of those games where we had a lot of fun and did a lot of things to mess with each other. It was a historical game as well as a hysterical game. On the last play of the game—and we were playing the width of the field, fifty-three yards, instead of the length of the field—Bud threw a forty-yard bomb to Terry Jastrow. The ball hit Terry right in the hands, then the chest, then the (groin area), then the knees—one of those passes that you finally drop, and we lost the game.

By this time, Bud was well into his fifties and he was supposed to be on his way to going to meet the president (Richard Nixon) before a game that Saturday at Pittsburgh. But he had taken a detour and flew into LaGuardia, where a bunch of us went out in a limousine to meet him so we could take him to the stadium to play that game of touch football. When Bud gets off the plane, he already has on his Gamecocks jersey under a blazer, and when he sees us, he rips off the blazer and says, "All right, let's go get those sons of b—!" He was fired up. We were in hysterics watching this, because there were so many people around us in the terminal seeing all this. For the game itself, we must have had about a hundred people out there, with lots of beer and stuff like that on the sidelines.

⊙〰〰〰⊙

Another of Wilkinson's many post-football endeavors was the Coach of the Year Clinics that he co-founded with Duffy Daugherty, which were coaching workshops held every year in various cities around the country. Notre Dame coach **Ara Parseghian** *was among the many big-name coaches who took part in some of the popular clinics:*

They took whoever was the coach of the year or someone else who had had a great year and put together a tour around the country of these various football clinics. I was involved with some of these for a few years, and that allowed me to get to know Bud a little better.

While we were on the road doing these clinics, we had time to socialize during the evenings, and we were able to exchange ideas. And we had our share of animated political discussions. That's because we were on the opposite sides of the fence in terms of political interests. Bud had run for U.S. senator in Oklahoma, been involved with the President's Council on Physical Fitness, and had gotten to know (Richard) Nixon. I had a huge disagreement with him about Nixon once. I felt, as evidenced by what took place at Watergate, that he (Nixon) was dishonest and had lied to the American people, and I felt very strongly about it. Of course, Bud felt just as strongly the other way. As it turned out, not that I'm gloating about it, but Nixon did resign. There was a value system that he had violated as far as the responsibilities of the president of the United States.

One thing about Bud during that discussion: I don't remember him ever actually raising his voice. He would make a forceful point with some emphasis, but I don't remember him raising his voice. You knew exactly where he was coming from. These were friendly discussions.

⊙﹏⊙

Andy Sidaris gets back to the subject of ABC's coverage of college football, starting with production preparation:

We prepared them pretty much as well as announcers are prepared now in terms of going over the game plan with them and discussing about how we would key in on certain players. I wrote a fourteen-page pamphlet on how to cover college football, to include drawings of the field and where cameras should be positioned as well as how to show highlights at halftime.

We would sit down and talk to Bud and Chris (Schenkel), and then Keith (Jackson), about how we were going to do the coverage. Then again, your coverage is only as good as the game you get. If you get a lousy game, your coverage is going to be seen as mediocre. We were fortunate to have a lot of great games in those days, such as the Notre Dame-Michigan State 10-10 tie in 1966 and Texas's victory over Arkansas in 1969, when those teams were ranked one-two. That was back when you had only one game that day, not five games like they do now.

As a director, I would try to be smooth. Chris Schenkel was smooth as the play-by-play guy and Bud was smooth as the color commentator, where now the announcing style is like a game of Nintendo. They give you five replays, a bunch of quick-flipped graphics, frequent zoombacks, and all this music. They jam it down your throat. I don't feel like I'm watching a football game anymore.

We never did any of the Nintendo-like stuff. We tried to put you in the ballpark. We would show the guy selling hot dogs, a cheerleader, or the emotion of one fan's face that told the story of what was going on down on the field—but no shots of sleeping babies or owners in their private boxes, or frequent reaction shots from coaches, as if those really mean anything. When I walk away, I feel like I've been watching a pinball machine and not a ball game.

❧

After retiring as Notre Dame coach following the 1974 season, **Ara Parseghian** *segued into some college football work himself, following a path that Wilkinson had trekked years earlier:*

Bud was a calm voice of reason. He did a number of Notre Dame games with Chris Schenkel while I was at Notre Dame. There was one game in particular, and I can't recall which game it was, when there was a huge outcry from Notre Dame fans accusing Bud of being real prejudiced against Notre Dame in how he analyzed the game. It might have been a Southern Cal game or a Michigan State game, I can't recall, except I know it wasn't the 1966 game against Michigan State in which we tied them, 10-10.

Soon after the game, (Notre Dame athletic director Moose Krause) came to me and said, "Boy, we are really hearing it from our fans." I said, "Well, let's sit down and look at a replay of the game so we can see and hear what they're talking about." So Moose and I sat down and looked at the tape of that whole game. When we were done watching it, we looked at each other and said, "Wow, where are these fans coming from with their complaints?"

Other than perhaps interpreting a positive comment about the other team—which is something you want to say when they do do well—or a critical comment against your team when you don't so something well—which he did for both sides—Moose and I mutually agreed that there really wasn't anything in how Bud analyzed the game that could be construed as bias against Notre Dame.

Bud was a pioneer for televised college football. Prior to that time, I can't recall a televised game where they had a permanent color-commentator guy. What I recall is Paul Christman, who had been at Missouri, doing color commentary on pro football, although he might also have done a few college games. But I remember Bud as the first permanent guy on color for the college game. It grew from there, and everything from has since improved dramatically in terms of how the game is covered and analyzed. In those days, you moved pieces around to show how plays were run, where today you have all this technology that takes you to a whole new level in how the games are broken down and replayed. Now you can draw on the screen exactly what has happened. They didn't have the replay capability on TV that you have today, where you can freeze a play while explaining to the viewer what they need to be looking at.

Barry Switzer offers up an interesting story that features someone other than Wilkinson, but at least involves the former Oklahoma coach:

The first time I ever saw Bud Wilkinson was as a punch line to another story. I went to Oklahoma in 1966 as an assistant to Jim McKenzie and went to a coaches' clinic that year in Chicago.

A good buddy of mine dating back to high school was Larry Lacewell, who was coaching at Kilgore Junior College. Before joining McKenzie, I had been coaching at Arkansas for about seven years, while Larry had been at Arkansas State and some other places, just kind of moving around. As it turned out, we would later hire Larry at Oklahoma, which was his move to big-time college football.

Kilgore didn't have much of a budget, so Lace couldn't afford to go to the Chicago clinic, but I told him that he could stay with me in my room, but getting there was up to him. I don't remember how Larry got to Chicago, but he finally did. Sometime later we were sitting around a bar at the Hilton Hotel, which I think was the largest hotel in the world at that time. All of us coaches were in there drinking some beer, and there's Lacewell, who's had a few pops, bragging about the fact that he's from Fordyce, Arkansas. Coach "Bear" Bryant also was from Fordyce, and Larry kept talking about how he and Coach Bryant were big buddies and how he had been Coach Bryant's number-one gofer at Alabama while getting his master's there. Lace would drive Coach Bryant to Birmingham and pick him up when he got back home on the train—stuff like that.

The more Larry drank, the more he bragged. Finally, I said to Larry, "You know, Coach Bryant is staying right across the street at the Blackstone, and he's got a suite over there." Other coaches had told me that, and, of course, every time a Coach Bryant or Coach (Woody) Hayes or somebody like that would walk through the lobby, all the other coaches would be following them with their eyes. I said, "Y'all are such big buddies, I'll find out what his suite number is, and then we can just go over there and see Coach Bryant." And Larry says, "Hell, yeah, let's go do it."

We cross over the street to the hotel, go up the elevator, and walk down the long hall to his door. We're standing there and I say, "Well, go ahead and knock, Larry. It's Coach Bryant's room." You could hear a lot of talking and laughter going on in there. Larry's just standing there trying to figure out what to say and to compose himself. I say, "You damn coward. If you don't knock on the door, I'm going to knock the hell out of it." About that time, the damn door opens, and it's Duffy Daugherty with the ice bucket in his hands. Now you've got to remember Duffy, who was always a great guy with an outgoing personality. He says, "Hey, guys, why don't you go fill this up with ice before you come in."

We took that ice bucket, went down the hall and filled it with ice, then came back to the room, and we were the bartenders in there for the rest of the night. Woody Hayes was in the room. Bud Wilkinson, Duffy Daugherty, Bob Devaney—they were all in there with Coach Bryant, and we fixed drinks all night long. We were like little flies on the wall listening to all their stories and BS.

"Coach, would you like another drink?"

"Yup."

They didn't even know who the bartenders were. Hey, they wouldn't remember us. Besides, they were half-drunk by the time we got there. As far as they knew, we could just as well have been part of the hotel room service. But, yeah, Coach Bryant was glad to see Larry and he did his best to make him feel comfortable. He asked him how his mama was, because he (Coach Bryant) used to date his (Lacewell's) mama. Every now and then, I still look at Larry and say, "Damn, Larry, you kind of remind me of Coach Bryant, you know that?" I love busting his chops over that. And, oh yeah, that was the first time I ever saw and got to talk to Bud Wilkinson.

❧

Curt Gowdy offers this nutshell summation of Wilkinson's TV work:

Bud didn't do any TV while I was down there (1946-49); they didn't even have television in Oklahoma City. It came in two or three years after I left. But I already knew how intelligent a guy he was; very glib. I knew he could be good on the air, even though he never had what I would call a great voice. He talked sort of low, kind of quiet.

❦

Gowdy recalls a story involving one of Wilkinson's former star players at Oklahoma, Darrell Royal—a story Gowdy relayed to Royal while the former was televising a game for ABC in 1961:

When I went down to Austin to do the Thanksgiving weekend Texas-Texas A&M game for ABC in 1961, I told Darrell (Royal) a story from his days playing at Oklahoma. I had also broadcast Darrell when he was a halfback at Oklahoma back in the late forties. If you check the starting lineup of that '49 team, I think you will find that seven or eight of the eleven went on to become head coaches. Guys like Jack Mitchell, Darrell Royal, and Jimmy Owens. They were outstanding guys, not just football players.

Darrell and I went out to dinner and I told him: "I'll never forget the night that you guys played TCU in Fort Worth, Texas, while Dutch Meyer was at TCU. Bud had come to me and said, 'Man, this coaching can be tough. Darrell weighed only 165 or 170 when he came to me, and he was very unhappy because I took him out of the game.' So Bud took Darrell out of the game and put this sophomore, Lindell Pearson, who weighed about 210, in to take Darrell's place. Bud continued: 'Darrell came up to me on the sideline and wanted to know why he wasn't playing. He was very unhappy. I said, "Darrell, this is a very physical team, and I've got to have some power out there." And this Pearson kid took them right down the field and scored, and Oklahoma went on to beat TCU. He had a great game in the second half.'

"Bud said, 'Darrell was very unhappy and gave me hell, and I had to talk to him after the game.'"

This was the story I told Darrell, and he said, "Yeah, I remember that, and I was unhappy. But you know what? It taught me a great lesson about coaching. When these players get their feelings hurt or get mad or whatever, they're not getting enough minutes perhaps, but I learned how to handle situations like that because I can remember how Bud handled me. I learned that lesson from him."

∽⠀⠀⠀⠀⠀∽

Geoff Mason was part of the ABC Sports team that injected a new flair into college football telecasts. Mason began as a production assistant in the late sixties and eventually rose through the ranks to succeed the renowned Roone Arledge as executive producer of ABC Sports:

Chris Schenkel wrote the book on infusing the enthusiasm of a football stadium into his commentary. It wouldn't play that well today, but it played great in those days. He was not a journalist; he was a host—he was your eyes and ears in the stadium, and he was smart enough to know that that involved more than X's and O's.

He and Bud always had clearly defined roles, and those were well understood and hardly ever violated. Chris didn't get into the X's and O's, and Bud didn't get into the ambiance of the stadium. I think the viewer was always comfortable listening to two announcers that had those clearly defined roles. There was no confusion, and it was easy listening. You got a sense not only of what was going on in the stadium, with fur coats and big blankets on the knees, but you also understand what the six-foot-six, 270-pound senior offensive guard sidelined with a broken leg was going through. It was all part of a package, and it was the first time the fan got a sense of the experience as well as the game.

With Bud you got the smooth analysis with a low-key enthusiasm for the game that conjured up images of the old-time fan with the raccoon coat and pennant watching and cheering on his or her team. Announcers can't do that anymore because they have to be, quote-unquote, journalists. It was a different time.

They both took very good care of the sponsors, such as Chevrolet. Today that would seem like pandering. In those days, we were all a team—the schools, the conferences, the broadcasters, the sponsors. We were all in it together.

⟨∞⟩

When ABC put its announcing team in place after having reacquired the rights to college football starting in 1966, the trio was Chris Schenkel doing play-by-play, Wilkinson providing the analysis, and **Bill Flemming** *adding a spark as a sideline reporter. Flemming:*

My relationship with Bud was really divided into three parts. When I was doing play-by-play, he was still a coach. Then when he came on board with ABC in 1966, I was doing the on-the-field stuff. Then in later years, I worked two seasons with Bud on the Freedom Football Network, where he was the color man and I was the play-by-play guy. So I got to know him pretty well—I knew him for the better part of twenty-five years.

Bud was a very private person. When I say I knew him, I don't really know if I ever really did know him. He was very professional, certainly very gracious and a gentle person. He was always well focused on whatever we did. Once the shows were over, he departed and I wouldn't see him until the next week. We never really did socialize much, although I had my own plane at that time and, occasionally, I would drop him off wherever I could. I think he was in Saint Louis at that time. I probably got to know him more in the airplane than I did anyplace else.

Bud had a unique approach to being a color man. For instance, we were in Birmingham one time for the Alabama-

Auburn game, and Bear Bryant had a suite at a hotel. He invited Chris, Bud, and me over to have dinner with him. Chris and I were chuckling because once we got together, Bud and Bear were talking in all of this football language, and we could hardly hear what Bear was saying because he was talking in that low, deep voice of his. We needed an interpreter. They talked like that for an hour or so, by which time Chris and I had eaten our dinner. We got up to leave and to head back to our hotel, and Bud and Bear were still back there talking football.

⟡⟡⟡

Flemming explains Bud's role on the telecast:

Bud could be the most technical person, yet when he got on the air he was able to simplify things for the viewer. That was his greatest forte: He was a born teacher. He really enjoyed conveying information, and he was quite soft-spoken in doing so.

Some of this could be pretty complex stuff. When you take eleven men on an offense, and each man has to do something extremely important with very little tolerance for error, it requires a lot of tech talk that only coaches and players can understand. People today might wonder why it takes a coach so long to install, say, the West Coast offense, like what new coach Jon Gruden is doing in Tampa Bay (with the Buccaneers). The reason is that football is a very technical game, and learning the new terminology of a particular offense can take a very long time. Guys who can refine that and distill it into terms that the average person can really understand are special, and Bud was one of the best at doing that. That was his greatest asset.

He would never get really excited. The extent of his enthusiasm might be his saying, "You know, Chris, I think that was the best football play that I've seen this year." He wasn't one of those screaming, hyper color men like, unfortunately, we have today. It seems today that dead air is an anathema to any color commentary. They can't seem to stand having a moment of silence. With Bud, if there wasn't anything significant with the play or the trend going on in the game at the time, he wouldn't say anything. That was a relief, a lesson that people should learn from. But today, ego has gotten to a point where a guy has to have so much of what I call "playing time" on the air. My mute button is nearly worn out. Bud knew his place and he was a keen observer of what was going on.

He also had an uncanny way of seeing things developing and knowing what was going to happen before it did, almost like a premonition. We did a little on-location segment for the Freedom Football Network called "Keys to Victory." It was a fifteen-minute piece before every game. Ninety percent of the time he was right on the mark. And whenever he offered anything during a replay, he never stated the obvious like a right guard pulling and providing a key block. He would say something like, "This was set up two plays previous to this, where they faked (a particular thing) and then they came back two plays later and showed the real deal." It really took some intellect to be able to fully appreciate what Bud was saying.

༺❦༻

*While it's easy to think of Wilkinson as a pioneer in the role of coach-turned-commentator, **Flemming** remembers it as being a fairly common phenomenon:*

I don't recall ever working with someone who was an analyst who wasn't a former coach or player. When ABC got the college football telecasts in 1960 and 1961, I worked with Ray

Bud helps wife Mary with the dishes.

Elliott, who had been the coach at Illinois. Then it went to CBS, where I did games with Frankie Albert, who was a former player. I also did it with Davey Nelson, Ara Parseghian, and Frank Broyles. Frank was really good, and I also enjoyed working with Ara a lot because he brought a lot of reminiscences into the telecast. Bud was reluctant to reminisce a lot, and I think a lot of that had to do with his being such a private person. Modesty might be the better word: He was never one you could accuse of patting himself on the back.

We would go to media parties on the Friday nights before games, and Bud would always get bugged about his winning streak at Oklahoma and how it got stopped at Notre Dame. I sensed that he was uncomfortable at those times talking about himself and his teams. He was more a forward-thinking person, always thinking about where the sport of football was going and how it was developing. Remember, he had taken the Split-T offense of Don Faurot to Oklahoma with him and did a lot to develop it there, eventually to varying forms. He had a lot of inventiveness about him.

❦

TV sports veteran announcer **Curt Gowdy** *remembers Paul Christman and Wilkinson as being special talents as coaches-turned-commentators:*

There were very few of those guys then who were good enough to do what Paul and Bud were doing. Now they all take speech lessons in high school. They all want to be broadcasters now once they get through playing ball. Johnny Lujack was also a good color man—he did some games with the Giants. More and more the ex-coach and ex-athlete came into the picture—"jockitis" as (Howard) Cosell would call it. He hated them. I didn't mind them. I couldn't have gotten a better guy than Christman to work with. Then later I worked with Al Derogatis. He was terrific, a guy who had been an All-American center at Duke.

❦

Andy Sidaris *offers further assessment of Wilkinson's TV work:*

Bud's voice was a little low, but he made a lot of good points for us. When he analyzed a play, it really wasn't superb, but it was quite good.

What you had with Bud was an authority figure who you believed. He had great credibility. I think he was about the best coach who ever walked, and he knew how to explain things so well. He was in a league of his own, light-years ahead of everyone else both offensively and defensively when he was coaching, and he had a way of rallying people around him. He was a motivator.

When you hit town with Bud, it was like the world's fair had arrived. No one had more charm or was able to get more respect, doing all this with such confidence and personality. He was smiling, laughing, joking, wonderful, kind, and courteous. I can't imagine anyone being a better man than he.

With Bud, you got a solidifying, sensitive announcer without going overboard. Bud helped us maintain that nice college spirit, and that's important to a telecast. He did his homework and worked hard, and he made us all proud.

ominy

Geoff Mason can't look back at ABC's college football television coverage in the sixties and seventies, with Wilkinson et al. on board, without feeling that they were the good ol' days:

For a while we had one game and that was it. When we came into town, we were a big deal. We worked hard to do our homework, and at varying levels we had wonderful cooperation most everywhere we went. Those were some of the best days I've ever been involved with, and I've been doing this for over thirty years. Maybe those were the best days I've had in sports television. That's because it wasn't polluted by excessive financial considerations such as rights fees, which were nothing compared to what is being shelled out today. The industry hadn't become quite so serious. It was still raw and fun, and we were loving every week.

There weren't that many great teams back then—you didn't have the parity that you have now. Going into any season, it was a fairly predictable marketplace. You knew every year that you were going to do Texas-Oklahoma, Michigan-Michigan State,

Ohio State-Michigan, USC-UCLA—you could rattle off before
the season started what 60 percent of your televised schedule
would be, it was just a matter of when. It wasn't quite the challenge that it is now: Some people think that's better and some
people think it's worse. It all depends on your perspective.

I would get in Thursday night in time to have some dinner
and have some fun in the small college town, whether it was
Ann Arbor or State College or wherever. Having been there
many times before, we had friends in those communities, and
Friday was all about setting up, hooking up the cameras and
the microphones and the graphics machine, and getting the
copy organized. In those days we had to dictate copy over the
phone from New York, and maybe use the school's sports information director's typewriter to type in changes or the new
copy. Then midafternoon Friday we might have a two-hour
meeting during which we would go through it all, from how we
would come on the air, what players we were going to feature,
what the replay patterns were going to be, what biographical
information we would feature, what our graphic and numerical
analysis would be, what our editorial focus was going to be,
what our commentary trends would be in a vacuum going into
the game.

∽☙

*The sixties saw the dawning of a new age in sports television, with
ABC Sports and its bright yellow blazers signifying a sense of risk
and inventiveness, taking the stodge out of televised games. That
was indicative of the Roone Arledge school of thought, where game
telecasts encompassed much more than the game itself. It was when
entertainment and drama began to seep into sports coverage, as
was the case with what would become the enduringly popular* Wide
World of Sports. **Mason**:

At ABC Sports we were kind of setting the trend in the industry, and, other than Andy Sidaris, we all took it very seriously, and thank goodness he didn't because that's where the fun came.

We knew then because of what Roone Arledge and Chuck Howard had taught us, that we had to be prepared. You were nothing without preparation. That was one of the first lessons I learned there and it served me well there for thirty years. It's the same thing I teach kids here today at ESPN. If you're going to try to wing it, you have no chance to succeed. None. Don't even try. You're not going to fake anybody out in this business, because if you blow it, hundreds of thousands, if not millions, see it.

During the weekend of a game, Friday was all about preparation, and Saturday, basically, was final rehearsal and just do it. The most important part about the weekend was the getaway. We would spend hours organizing the getaway, and it involved the times, police escorts, and even helicopters, Lear jets, limos, or chartered planes occasionally—whatever it took to get us to the assignment or to just get home at a decent time.

I think production teams these days still feel the same spirit and sense of teamwork: I don't suggest what we did in those days was better, but I think it was more fun because every game was more special. Now they do more telecasts in three months than we did in a whole year. They're always on the air, so the pressures and the stressors are different.

In real candor, we weren't real concerned about budgets in those days. ABC Sports was doing really well, and no one was hassling us about budgets. Today, the CPA knows every penny. We were riding a crest of a wave in those days at ABC Sports. It was an exploding industry and it's like we were like surfers on our surfboards, just trying like hell to hold on for dear life. Everything we did was new, innovative, important, successful, fun, stressful, and heady. It was a great time to be in the business, and it will never be the same because there will never be another organization like ours that was setting new standards every time we woke up in the morning. Everything we did was new: satellites, foreign telecasts, isolated replays on the offensive guard in football.

～～～

Mason talks about how a competitive atmosphere at ABC motivated competing producers to try to outdo one another:

There would be a weekend where we would have like four or five regional games, and the producers would spend all week trying to figure out how to make their telecasts look better than Chuck Howard's. You didn't have much flexibility once the game started: Everyone had the cameras, the microphones, the slow-mo replays, and all that. But where you could make a difference was with things like the pregame show, how you introduced the players, and all that kind of ancillary stuff.

One time Roger Goodman and I were doing like the fifth regional game on a particular Saturday, and this was like the first game he and I had ever produced. We wanted to make a statement, and we were doing a game with the University of Houston at the Astrodome. I don't remember who the opponent was. We spent the better part of a month organizing, formatting, and getting set for our pregame show, which was like twelve minutes long.

We had to convince the Astrodome people to give us a separate booth so that we could put our announcers in there. We had couches and easy chairs and flowers, and it was the most magnificently produced pregame show ever, and we were so proud of it. We went into the station break patting ourselves on the back and high-fiving each other all around. Great job, everybody.

Now we get set for the game out of the station break, and on the opening kickoff the guy runs it back ninety-five yards for a touchdown. The opening kickoff. I talk to Roger and ask, "Okay, what do you have?" And he says, "Have what?" Not good. So we had a terrific pregame show, but it would have been nice to catch the ninety-five-yard runback. But that wasn't high on our priority list because that's not how we were going to make our mark back in the office on Monday morning.

Those kinds of things happened every week, and there was only so much you could do to impress your boss. But in all honesty, that was the kind of thinking out of the box that allowed *Monday Night Football* to become so good, people reaching beyond themselves.

I can remember using black gloves in those telecasts so my hands wouldn't get put on the air. We used to do all of our graphics with little magnetic letters—we used to have to build them with our hands on these little black magnetic boards. A camera would look at that board and only see the white letters and numbers. As I'm speaking now, I'm looking at CNN, and they do more with graphics in a minute than I would do in six months. That's because it's all done now by computer. You have color, backgrounds, and they move and they blink and they pulsate and they change—I never cease to be amazed by how much more sophisticated the onscreen product is today compared to what we had to do thirty years ago. Even the uneducated viewer can notice how far we've come.

Like I said, we were taught to think outside the box. We did some things that were innovative and we did some things that were stupid. We were always reaching. We had a young bunch of people that kept striving to do better, that no matter how much credit we got or how many accolades we received, we just kept pouring it back into the product. We were totally oriented to what was on the screen, and we would stop at nothing to try and improve the quality of the product. Arledge taught us how we were all about telling stories on the screen. We never took ourselves for granted and tried never to get lazy. It predicated a time with some ugly yellow blazers and goofy features.

CRWLS

ABC had a "secret sauce" that gave its game telecasts a different flavor, which **Bill Flemming** *tries to explain:*

I think we broadened the base. From a technical standpoint, we added cameras, such as cameras in the end zone and on the sidelines. This took a lot of doing because the universities and the coaches were worried about how these might obstruct the views of many of the fans sitting in the stands.

There was a man at ABC by the name of Jules Barnathan who was the head of all technical stuff, and he was a genius in getting all this done. Then there was the creative ability of Roone Arledge. He knew he wanted to get more of the sounds of college football: He had microphones placed in different spots, and did some things with camera angles. Since we now had more technical capabilities, there were more things that we could do during a telecast such as coming down onto the field with me, even if they couldn't always get me on camera—at least they could get something like a live injury report.

Also at that time we installed a system where people in New York keeping track of other games had an open line to me. I could get a hot score or some other piece of breaking information that I could interject during the telecast. Instead of flashing a score superimposed onto the screen, like Ohio State 10, Michigan 7, I could say that so-and-so scored for Ohio State on such-and-such a play with a minute and a half left to go in the half. There was more meat to it than just the stuff that was scrolled.

Overall, we were simply expanding for the viewer what he could see and hear in the course of watching the game. We also had a postgame setup where we could flip it back to New York for a few minutes once the game was finished; then, in keeping the line open, they could send it back to us for a postgame wrap-up that might include a short interview with the winning coach or something like that. Before, with other networks, it was just meat and potatoes. When the game was over, it was more like, Okay, that's it; the game is over, goodbye.

ABC milked it, and cross promotions during the week helped, too. We also did a lot more regionalizing with games, which helped tremendously in terms of broadening the audience. We were innovative, just as we were with *Wide World*, and look at how many people in television have followed that format.

༺ﮩ٨ﮩﮩ٨ﮩ༻

Flemming continues his look back by analyzing what went on in the booth before and during the broadcasts:

Chris was one of the best lead announcers there ever has been, and he knew how to leave the door open for Bud.

Bud's contributions in the production sense were very important. He was the guy who could lead the producer and the director in the direction that we ought to go. Also, because of the confidences that coaches involved in the game being covered placed in Bud—knowing that we weren't going to reveal anything—we were prepared to know what the coach probably would do, say, in a certain third-and-eight situation.

We knew beforehand where we would be going in our production, and it was a matter of trying to be a step ahead of everybody else. Maybe that was one of the subtleties injected into our telecasts that set them apart from other college football telecasts that viewers had grown accustomed to. You could always go to the fifty-yard-line wide shot and be saved, but that was the easy way to do it. You needed to be willing to gamble a lot, although we didn't see much of those other kinds of shots as gambles because most of what Bud had presented in those production meetings turned out to be true.

Our production meetings on Friday afternoon were pretty extensive. Chuck Howard was the producer and Andy Sidaris the director. We always scheduled them late in the afternoon, because earlier, the three of us would be with the coaching staff watching video. Then we would have the production meeting around five o'clock, and it would last about two hours. It was pretty well structured.

Chuck would have in his mind what the story line of the game was, and then throw it open as to who the key guys would be for close-ups and what each of the three of us was supposed to do. On Saturday we would show up and all that was left to do really was to check the mikes, and 90 percent of the time they wouldn't work. We had a lot of technical problems, but from the production standpoint we were well organized.

Andy got along great with the camera crew, which was critical to the telecast. He would always be telling the cameramen, "Sell me on your next shot. Sell me. Find something that looks interesting and then go in on it."

Flemming:

The most memorable game to me that the three of us did together was Oklahoma-Nebraska in 1971. Nebraska won, 35-31. Everything that had been planned turned out to be true.

Another one was the 1969 Arkansas-Texas game for number one. President Richard Nixon was there. I remember interviewing him in the locker room—that was wild. But we had that one well organized, too, with cameras in both locker rooms to be sure at least that we had the winning locker room covered.

I can remember that morning how the fog was right down on the treetops. This was in Fayetteville. We were staying in some big, beautiful place about twenty miles from the football stadium. Helicopters were to pick us up there, and being a pilot I was very nervous about it because it was treacherous flying with such low visibility in that fairly mountainous terrain. We got in okay and landed on a practice field next to the stadium. We then sweated out the arrival of the president, and, by golly, here he came, out of the clouds in his helicopter.

Arkansas went ahead, 14-0, in the game, and then Texas scored and went for two. That made it 14-8. Texas then scored again and kicked the extra point to make it 15-14, Texas.

Those two games really had tremendous impact on ABC's coverage of college football.

I also did the Ohio State-Michigan game in 1969, which was Bo Schembechler's first clash against Ohio State and Woody Hayes. That was Bo's first year at Michigan, and Ohio State was supposed to have the team of the century. The Buckeyes were a twenty-one-point favorite, but Michigan beat them, 20-12. I did the play-by-play for that game because Bud and Chris had gone to California to do USC-UCLA, which usually fell on the same day as Ohio State-Michigan. I was originally scheduled to do that USC-UCLA game because it was of lesser importance, until two or three weeks before the end of the season it became apparent that this was going to be a blowout at Michigan. They didn't want to get stuck with that game for their first-string guys, Chris and Bud.

You've got to remember in those days that there wasn't a proliferation of college football because of the controls the NCAA had over the number of appearances each year that schools could make on television, either nationally or regionally. There were all kinds of numerical juggling of balls to try to get the best games each week without violating that NCAA rule. Now, you can practically get any game, anywhere, that you want to. I think the product has been watered down a lot.

⚬⚭⚬

Chuck Howard, ABC's college football producer at the time—now deceased—once gave his own version of what set ABC's telecasts of college football apart from what had been previously produced:

You have to keep the audience updated. For instance, maybe we'd mention at the top of the telecast that Oklahoma had lost both their offensive tackles and this was going to be a problem. There's a tendency to assume everybody's heard that, but that obviously isn't true. People pick up the telecast in progress. So I'd mention that to Chris (Schenkel). Or maybe the weather had changed, and I'd want Chris to talk about that.

With Bud, I'd say—and he would be the only one who could hear me—"Bud, I don't understand why Kansas continues to try to run into a stacked front. They have to throw the ball or screen or something." If Bud thought I was off base or the comment didn't warrant anything, he'd just forget about it. But if it did warrant something, he'd pick it up in his own words. . . . Sometimes we'd talk during the commercials. I'd say something like, "What could Woody Hayes be thinking of in this situation?" and he'd pick it up.[6]

⚬⚭⚬

Chris Schenkel:

Woody Hayes really admired Bud. At one Ohio State-Purdue game, we were staying at the same hotel as Ohio State. Bud and I arrived about the same time Woody did. Woody just handed him his game plan right there in the lobby. He said, "Here, Bud, here's what we're going to do."

We went to our rooms, and Bud was looking the plan over and trying to explain it to me. About an hour later, there's a knock on the door and it's Woody. He said, "Bud, we're about the same age, and you know my mind slips from time to time and yours probably does, too. I'm just a little afraid you might leave that game plan on your desk when you and Chris go out for dinner. Do you mind if I take it back?"

I told Bud later, "It's got nothing to do with your memory. Woody just remembered I'm a Purdue grad."[7]

⌒⌒⌒

Terry Jastrow was in those days a production assistant to Chuck Howard at ABC:

I loved the games when Bud was really close to the other coaches. In those days, the Duffy Daugherty, John McKay, Darrell Royal, or Frank Broyles games were great, because Bud would take Schenkel and Howard and me to meetings or dinners; he saw we were included. You really got to know the big coaches like Bear Bryant. You were calling him Bear ten minutes into the event because that's what Bud called him.

Sometimes, coaches like Daugherty or Woody Hayes would gather their teams at the end of practice and they'd get Bud to say a word. I'll tell you, it was Knute Rockne returned. He was quiet, powerful, and direct, and those guys were jumping through their uniforms when he got done. He'd say stuff like, "This is the opportunity you live your life for, this is what you play a sport for, this is what athletics is all about. It's a question of being a man, being all you can be, focusing on the positive." You were ready to suit up and go play yourself by the time he got done with one of those speeches.[8]

⟨✦⟩

Andy Sidaris:

One time after I had been married just a short time, Bud and Chris Schenkel came out to my house just to have a drink and chat some. My mother was there and she later told me, "He made me feel like a young woman again." That's how charming, sweet, and nice he was, and he was that way with everybody. People just loved being around him.

⟨✦⟩

Geoff Mason expounds some more on game-day coverage, with a twist, at ABC:

Andy Sidaris invented what we used to call the cheesecake shots. He brought that perspective to our coverage with Arledge's support, and that was "Capture the feeling in the stadium." And you can't do the stadium unless you show things like the cheerleaders, the people who go to the game with painted faces, and all the banners. We were the first ones to get off the playing field and onto the sidelines, so to speak. In so doing, we would go to great lengths to make little bits work with sideline announcers, such as Jim Lampley in those pre-Jack Arute days. In those days it was all new, and we would feature players, their families, and a few celebrities that happened to be there.

It was always a huge, huge problem organizing the bands with the television time-outs, the pregame show, the player intros and all that. We even wrote a production assistant's manual after a couple of years: *The Production Assistant's Manual for College Football, or How I Learned to Cue the Bird and Bury the Anthem.* That referred to an experience we had one time with the falcon at the Air Force Academy. We were all organized to cue the school's falcon, which was supposed to fly away at a certain point in the pregame activities. Whoever was on the sideline that day had arranged a cue in which he would raise his right arm to signal the academy folks that it was time to let the falcon go. Sure enough, five minutes before we go on the air, our guy on the sideline is getting himself organized and he gets an itch behind his right ear, scratches his ear, and away flies the falcon. That's it. Falcon was gone, disappeared over the Colorado hills. There were a million stories like that.

⟨✦⟩

Keith Jackson later took over play-by-play duties at ABC, putting him alongside Wilkinson for several years:

I worked with him three years. He was easygoing. Not greatly creative, really. Simple. Understood the basics of his job. This was typical Wilkinson. Once he understood the nomenclature of his job, that's what he did. He asked me one time about my basic philosophy when we started working together, and I said, "It's very simple: You amplify, qualify, and punctuate, and don't intrude." And by gum, that's the way that he worked. He simply told you why one team was winning and why one team was losing, or why one team might win or one team might lose. He pretty much left it at that.

He wasn't a comedian and didn't consider himself a particularly adroit entertainer. But he did prepare himself, maybe a bit less than some of the others I've worked with over the years, but sufficiently to satisfy the television viewer. If you remember back in the sixties and seventies, the viewing public wasn't quite as sophisticated in the lore and vernacular of football as it is now.

ᏳᎽᏒᏒᏃ

Jackson:

What has gone on in the industry across the years is that all of us have been forced to be more aggressive in pursuing and presenting information: All those toys we have now to play with, such as telestrators, are wonderful.

(Bob) Griese was the best one I've ever worked with. I worked with Bob for twelve years. He was as good as anyone in filling your chest with fact. Bob would send you home with a sackful where Bud sent you home only with what you needed. Spartan would be a good word.

The thing about Wilkinson, and about every great coach that ever lived, regardless of the sport—or every politician that had great success—when they walked into a room, you knew it. Everybody looked.

ᏳᎽᏒᏒᏃ

Jackson recalls one game in particular that he did with Wilkinson, mostly because it also included a third wheel by the name of Paul "Bear" Bryant:

One game I remember doing with Bud was the Liberty Bowl, and Paul Bryant was also doing the game with us. I can't remember who the teams were or what year it was, but I'll never forget how cold it was. It was bitter cold. I remember Paul being bundled up all night in a big ol' fur parka and ski mask, and he was right at home with his flask in his pocket.

They had catered some food in for us—ribs, and you could get great ribs in Memphis. We had a big feast before the game. We all ate and were then waiting around, and a producer was really beginning to fidget because Bear hadn't shown up yet. He didn't get there until about thirty minutes before rehearsal.

We go upstairs and we sit down, and Bryant didn't want anything to do with me. In that low mumble of his, he said something like, "I don't really like you, boy, so I'm going to sit over here off to the side with Bud and talk to him about the game." I said, "You go ahead, Coach. I don't give a damn what you do, just don't get in the way now because I'm going to have to tell the people who's winning and who's losing."

I think Paul had stopped by at about every other house on his way to the stadium to shake hands with somebody he knew, and he was pretty well greased by the time he got there. And that cold air didn't do him any good either. So he gets up there in the booth, and he and Bud are sitting a good ten to fifteen feet away from me. Bud was going to try to control Paul, getting him in and out of the commentary, and he worked hard at it all night. Every time Bud asked him a question about the game on the field, Paul would mumble in that low voice, "Errrr, uhhhh, welllll, let me think about that a minute." Meantime, three plays go by, and finally Paul would speak up and talk about something that had taken place three plays ago.

The whole night was like that, and Paul sort of started nodding off a bit late in the game. After the game Bud told me, "I never worked so damn hard in all my life." It was fun. I'm sure a videotape of that telecast exists somewhere. We had a lot of that stuff in the seventies and eighties, everybody from presidents and kings on down.

⚬⚬⚬

Flemming's memories of Wilkinson date back to before they ended up working together at ABC:

I did some of the Oklahoma-Nebraska games while Bud was still coaching the Sooners. I was doing one of the games in '61 or '62, and that was the first time I met him while he was still a coach.

I remember the game was in Norman because he had a party for us at his house. All the coaches were there and his wife, Mary, was such a gracious hostess. I just liked the whole atmosphere. Just the way he lived. He was able to have some kind of decent home life and he overcame a lot of personal tragedies, such as when he battled testicular cancer earlier in his life.

If I had to sum it all up, I would call him a groundbreaker in the sense that he was able to do the perfect kind of commentary, in that it showed restraint at the same time it brought to the viewer a sense of having learned something. Chris was the perfect announcer for him.

⚬⚬⚬

Flemming:

Toward the end, I watched Bud suffer a lot. I can remember the last game we did together on the Freedom Football Network, which involved the three service academies—Air Force, Navy, and Army. We had very good audiences.

This one time we were at Colorado Springs, which is at pretty high altitude, and we were climbing up to the press box, and Bud stopped at least two times on the way up. He looked really ashen. We got up there, and I said, "Coach, are you okay?" He said, "I don't know. I've been having some heart problems, and I don't know, this may be it." I said, "Hey, don't say that." And he said, "Well, I'm scheduled to go in for some tests. I just don't feel right."

I remember he was really down that day, energy-wise. He had driven with me from Denver to Colorado Springs, and I remember he was pretty quiet on the drive back. That's the last I remember working with Bud. Army had pulled out of the Freedom Football agreement, and that would be the last time we did one of those games.

It was a wonderful concept. The problem was that the academies became jealous of each other. Air Force had emerged superior among the three, and Army didn't like being exposed in such a way. Army had been accustomed to being on television only once a year, for Army-Navy, and now that they were on every third or fourth week and not playing well, they didn't like that.

Still, it was a nice way for Bud to end his broadcast days. One bonus to having Bud do games over the years was that everyone would practically genuflect when he walked into a dressing room or strolled across campus. And he was always very gracious and very personable. I really treasured his friendship a lot.

❧

Curt Gowdy, also a TV sports veteran, stayed in close touch with Wilkinson long after Gowdy left Oklahoma in 1949 to go call New York Yankees games:

After I went to New York to work with the Yankees, I didn't see much of Bud. One time I was in Washington, D.C., when he went up there to work for Nixon. He called me and invited me up to watch dinner while watching the (Apollo 11) moonshot. So we had dinner and then I went over to his apartment and watched the landing on the moon with him. I was there in Washington to broadcast baseball's All-Star Game. I think it was the one-hundredth birthday of baseball (1969).

That night I went home and my eyes were burning like hell. My eyes got so painful that I could hardly stand it. I went and got some ice and packed my eyes with washcloths, but that didn't help. I could hardly open them. My wife called downstairs and asked where the nearest hospital with an ophthalmologist was. She called a cab for me, and by this time I couldn't see. She helped me get on the elevator and then into the cab. It was about two or three in the morning, and I started to think that it must have been the wine I had with Bud, or something.

What had actually happened was that afternoon we (the NBC television crew) had been rehearsing for the All-Star Game, as well as a lot of on-field interviews being taped for the next day's telecast. I had been working in front of these lights up in the booth: I forget what kind of lights they were, but it was like looking into the sun. Those lights had burned the covering off of my retinas. I had a helluva time.

It just so happened that a friend of mine, a fellow fly-fisherman, was one of the best eye surgeons in America. My wife called him and he referred her to this guy to go see in Washington the next day. They gave me cortisone and packed my eyes. That night I went to a big dinner that I emceed wearing dark glasses. The pain had gone down, and as it turned out I was able to broadcast the game.

I'd go a long time without seeing Bud, and then every now and then I would run into him. He always knew how much I appreciated how much he had helped me.

❦

Barry Switzer talks more about his friendship with Wilkinson:

I got to know him after I became an assistant at Oklahoma because he still lived in Norman and came to some of the games and some of the social events. But we didn't become friends and business partners in oil and gas until after I had become head coach (in 1973). We did some oil and gas deals together. He was a partner with John David Davenport who lived in Edmond, Oklahoma, who made Bud millions of dollars.

Bud and I became friends and did things together, like going to Scottsdale and playing golf. He did some of our games on ABC with Chris Schenkel. One story is about the time that Bud, Chris, and Roone Arledge covered the first Peach Bowl, when they had that high-stepping, marching Florida A&M band. Bud told me the story.

They were getting ready to go live on the air, and they were doing a check-down to make sure everything was cued up and ready to go, with Roone Arledge back in New York and Chuck Howard and Chet Forte and all those guys out in the TV truck outside the stadium. Bud and Chris are up there in the announcers' booth with their yellow coats and all ready to go, with about sixty seconds to go before they went on the air. Chuck is talking to everyone on the entire crew scattered around the stadium and everything is set.

At one point he's talking to the guy down in the tunnel who's supposed to cue the band to come out at just the right time. The guy with the band is standing near the band director when Chuck calls down to the tunnel guy and asks him if he knows what his cue is and if he's ready. The guy says he is, but Chuck tells the guy to show him the cue—you see, Chuck is watching all this on a TV monitor in the truck. The guy turns around to the band director and asks him if he knows what the cue is and then gives him the cue just to check.

Well, that band starts off down the tunnel and onto that field, and Chuck Howard about has a heart attack yelling at the guy to stop them. They've gone out there too early. The guy in the tunnel runs after the band director telling him to stop the band, and the director yells back, "Stop them!? I don't have a signal for that!! I've only got the one to start them!!" There's no stopping them once they started, and they're going a hundred miles an hour.

Bud and Chris could hear this up in the booth and they're mortified. There's the band performing out there on the field, and when they go on the air Bud and Chris are having to scream to be heard above this loud noise with the band playing and the crowd going nuts, because they had an open-air booth. So there's Chris and Bud yelling at the top of their lungs to be heard, and a little later Chuck Howard's phone rings down in the truck. It's Roone Arledge calling from New York.

Chuck picks up the phone and he hears Roone asking, "Whose idea was it to have the band on the field playing at the same time we come on national television?" Chuck kind of gulps and pauses, and Roone says, "I'm going to tell you, this is really great!! It's the greatest damn atmosphere with excitement and enthusiasm that I've ever seen. I came out of my seat—that made me want to cover the kickoff!!" Bud said the whole thing was one of the most surprising, shocking, and funniest things he had ever been a part of in television. The thing was, Bud wasn't a yelling kind of guy. Welcome to the Peach Bowl!

∽∾

Eddie Crowder, *one of Wilkinson's many great quarterbacks at Oklahoma, was one of his former coach's favorite golfing partners in tournaments:*

Bud and I played golf a lot together and had some nice success together in tournaments. One time he invited me to play in a best-ball tournament in Washington, D.C., at Burning Tree Country Club, which we would win two out of the three times we played.

That week, I had a speaking engagement at a coaching clinic in New Jersey. Johnny Majors was the other speaker. Another guy was running the clinic, so I called and asked if Johnny and I could adjust the schedule as speakers so I could play in this golf tournament. I chartered a plane to fly me to Dulles Airport. Bud picked me up. We had a few refreshments to help us relax, and we won the tournament by three shots. We played the same tournament again two years later and then won it again after that, and we were sort of banned after that.

He was a delight to play golf with. He was a guy who could almost will it into the cup. He was a very good player. During those golf tournaments, he had such a wonderful, positive air about him all the time. He would say, "Hey, pard, I'm going to hit this three-wood right up close, snuggling the pin." We might be on a par-five hole, and by golly, he would hit it to within two or three feet. It was just astonishing. He had a way for doing unique things, and that included the golf course as well as the football field. He was a big Ben Hogan fan, and he used a lot of illustrations of Hogan in talking to the Oklahoma team.

∽∾

Keith Jackson:

One of my favorite stories that defines and reflects how and why Bud was a very good football coach comes from a time long after he had finished coaching at Oklahoma. He was fiddling around with one of those *Superstars* events we used to do down in Rotunda, Florida, involving celebrities, actors, writers, and so forth.

At one point, a Frenchman and an Englishman got into a big hassle over the rules after they had run a bicycle race, each contending he should have more points and that the other should be disqualified. They were almost to the point of fisticuffs. Bud, being the commissioner of these competitions, had been called in by Don Ohlmeyer to settle this dispute. I don't know if Bud knew anything about the rules in question, but out he comes with rules in hand and all of his usual dignity and enormous persona as he walked up to this conflict and said, "What is our problem?" They each screamed their version of it, after which he said, "Well, here are the rules," and he very quietly read the rules to them.

Now, mind you, here we were standing there in ninety-eight-degree heat, in the middle of the day, and the sunscreen is beginning to bubble just a little bit. Bud says, after reading the rules, "Those are the rules now, and if we can reach a gentleman's agreement within ninety seconds, then we'll be able to go on about our business and conclude the morning session. Otherwise, we will rerun the event." It took about twelve seconds before he got his deal, and Bud was last seen hanging his straw hat inside the air-conditioned truck and things went on.

That was kind of the way he managed and coached his football team.

Roger Wehrli was a defensive back with the Saint Louis Cardinals during Wilkinson's short tenure there as head coach in 1978 and 1979, which was enough time for him to see the class-act side of Wilkinson:

Bud was co-chairman with Barry Switzer of a golf tournament in Oklahoma City for the Society to Prevent Blindness. During that one off-season when Bud was still coaching the Cardinals, he invited me, Jim Hart, Dan Dierdorf, and our wives to the tournament. They sent a Lear jet to Saint Louis to pick us all up to spend a long weekend up there, and then they flew us back to Saint Louis. We stayed at the home of one of the big boosters there and we just had a great time. We got to know him real well off the field. That meant a lot to us. He was a great man, and it was just an honor to be around him.

6

PLAYING WITH THE CARDS DEALT

Fourteen years after stepping down as Oklahoma coach, Wilkinson returned to coaching in 1978 by accepting an offer from owner Bill Bidwill to coach the National Football League's Saint Louis Cardinals. Bidwill had just parted company with coach Don Coryell after a disappointing 7-7 season. He was looking for a big-name coach whose hiring would surprise people and, hopefully, stimulate a new sense of purpose for a team that was starting to fray at the edges.

It was a bold move by Bidwill, but a dubious one as well. Not only had Wilkinson been out of coaching for more than a decade, but he had no NFL experience. Besides, he was now on the high side of sixty. Many of his players were less than half his age and were being subjected to media criticisms that the game had passed the aging Wilkinson by.

By the time Wilkinson hit town, there were signs of trouble. Star running back Terry Metcalf had been unable to negotiate a new contract with the hard-line Bidwill and had left the Cardinals to go play in the Canadian Football League. Another key loss was right guard Conrad Dobler, who had been a key part of the Cardinals' strong offensive line, which was aging more and more by the hour—as were Cardinals at other key positions.

Between being an NFL neophyte, an aging coach regarded as over the hill by some players, losing key players, and stepping into a situation in which he would have little input in personnel decisions, Wilkinson was walking into trouble. It would be a short-lived venture, but one in which Wilkinson was able to touch a number of lives.

ᏩᎳᎳᎾ

Cardinals quarterback **Jim Hart** *wasn't surprised when he learned of Wilkinson's hire:*

When we learned that Bud had been hired to be the new Cardinals coach, the feeling pretty much was that this was (owner) Bill Bidwill's just doing the unexpected again. It was a surprise to everyone—fans, players, media. After a while, Bidwill doing the unexpected was to be expected. Every time the coaching position came open, we thought, Okay, what's he going to look for this time? Maybe he thought of all this as some sort of game. I never did discuss it with him. A lot of people took Bud to task because he had been out of the game for so long. They just thought that he would not be the guy for the job.

His reputation preceded him, and some of us who had been playing for a while knew who he was and what he had accomplished in the college ranks. But there were a number of younger players who never did appreciate him. There were media reports questioning Bud's suitability for the job, suggesting that the game had passed him by. Some of the younger players believed

what they were reading and hearing, and they never really gave
him the opportunity to prove what he could do.

⚬⚬⚬

Running back **Jim Otis** *recalls Wilkinson's hiring:*

As soon as he got the job with the Cardinals, he called a bunch
of us in, some of the mainstays. We met him over at his hotel
room, and he was very positive about what he had to say. He
was a legend. I had met Bud Wilkinson when I was in college
and he was doing some broadcasting. I was a big fan of his, and
now all of a sudden he's the coach. Bud always talked in
tremendous positives, and it was great knowing that you were
going to be associated with a coach like that.

⚬⚬⚬

Jim Hart *describes how the stage was set with the Cardinals upon
Wilkinson's arrival:*

Things were pretty well torn apart, mainly because of Don
Coryell's leaving. It was just a bad situation. Don had gotten fed
up with Bill (Bidwill). The catalyst for Don's leaving was Bill's
not wanting to negotiate with Terry Metcalf, who was pretty
much the franchise. Things had been so good in '74, '75, and
'76. Even in '77 we were right there in the hunt for a playoff spot
until late in the season. Seventy-eight and '79 were dismal, but
that's because we were decimated. Bud really inherited a skele-
ton crew left over from the good years of the mid-seventies.

Bud thought he would be around for a few years and would
have that time to put his team together. As it turns out, that
was not to be the case, either. Bill Bidwill and the scouting

department pretty much put the team together with little input from the coaching staff. I'm sure the coaching staff helped in compiling information about prospective players, but in terms of being involved in the decision process, that didn't happen for the coaches.

ᏀᎯᎯᎯᏬ

Whether he liked the situation or not, there was nothing **Hart** *could do about it:*

I had been in the NFL twelve or thirteen years by the time Bud got there. We didn't have the luxury of free agency in those days, where you could just say, "To heck with you guys" and go someplace else. You were stuck. It's not until after your career is finished and you look back when you can see how frustrating it was.

ᏀᎯᎯᎯᏬ

Hart *compares and contrasts Coryell and Wilkinson:*

Bud was quite different from Coryell. Don was excitable, and he motivated in a different way. I remember going to the sideline when it was something like third and one, and he would be yelling, "We're going to throw it! Throw it!" I'd say, "Well, Coach, we can run for the first down easily, and we've got two good running backs." And he'd still be saying, "Throw it! Throw it! Throw it!" Jim Hanifan would just look at me and whisper, "You know what to do."

We'd go back out to the huddle, call a running play, and make the first down. And then we would throw it. This was sort of what the Saint Louis Rams are doing now, and I'm sure Coryell is sitting down somewhere out on the West Coast watching the Rams and grinning from ear to ear, saying, "Man, this is what I always wanted to do back in the seventies, but it just wasn't acceptable to do that sort of thing back then." Actually, he did throw the ball more once he got to San Diego coaching the Chargers.

Bud told me from the start, "You've been playing professional ball for twelve or thirteen years now, and I'm not going to be the one to tell you about things." Our quarterback coach was Harry Gilmer, so Bud left those things up to Harry. Bud let his coaches coach, just as Don had. So from that standpoint he was easy to play for.

❦

Jim Hanifan, who as of 2002 was still in football as an assistant coach with the Saint Louis Rams, was a holdover from Coryell's staff, staying on as offensive line coach for Wilkinson's first year with the Cardinals. Hanifan:

Don Coryell, Joe Gibbs, and myself were among those on that staff before Bud's arrival, and it looked like we were all going off in different places.

When Bill Bidwill hired Bud, it was a shock not only to the Saint Louis community but also to the National Football League as a whole. He had been out of football for fourteen years and had been involved with politics in Washington, D.C., and this and that, and all of a sudden here he is in pro ball.

I had opportunities to leave there and join some other teams. I had a year left on my contract with the Cardinals and could have gotten out of it, but I thought, I'm not going to do that; I'm going to stay here for the year. And I'm so glad that I did that— that I decided to stay. It gave me the chance to be around Bud that year, and I so much enjoyed that year with him.

❦

Hanifan talks about helping Wilkinson make the adjustment to coaching in the NFL after his long layoff from coaching:

When Bud came to the Cardinals, he realized that he had been away from the game for fourteen years. Two, this was not college football; it was pro football. Three, the game itself, even at the college level, had evolved somewhat through those fourteen years. There were some fundamentals that we could still all agree about, thinks like blocking and tackling that will probably never change. But so much of the stuff had changed radically. Bud realized that he had a lot to learn. What he did was rely on the rest of us who had been coaching at the pro level for a while.

Two of the offensive coaches from Don's staff were still with the team, that being Harry Gilmer and myself. On the defensive side of the ball, he hired guys who also had plenty of pro experience, such as Tom Bettis, who had been the defensive coordinator with the Kansas City Chiefs. What Bud did simply was to assume the role as head coach and delegate all of the various duties to his assistant coaches. He wasn't about to do it all by himself. He knew better.

❦

*Cardinals defensive back **Roger Wehrli**, on Wilkinson:*

We had heard a lot about him. He was a legend. Of course, we had just had a coach that we really loved—Don Coryell. He left Saint Louis on kind of bad terms. He really was a players' kind of coach, and we had a good team under him. He and Bidwill hadn't gotten along well that previous year.

It was neat having Bud come in; I really enjoyed having him here. Bud also was a likable coach from the players' standpoint. He went to bat for us with the ownership and wanted to do a lot of things with the Cardinals that he was never allowed to accomplish. It was a frustrating time, too, because he didn't get a chance to implement the kind of program he wanted to implement.

⚬━━━⚬

Wehrli *talks about what set Wilkinson apart from Coryell:*

Things didn't really change that much for us on defense while he was here. The most significant change was just in how he handled the team. Coryell was a really fiery type of individual, where Bud was more of the laid-back type of coach.

There are two different head-coaching philosophies in football. Some of the head coaches are very hands-on right there on the field at the different positions—Coryell was one of those kinds of coaches, especially with the offense. With the defense, he just left it up to the assistants. The coach I had in college, Dan Devine at Missouri, was more a stand-back-and-watch-the-players type of coach who would evaluate players from a distance and let the assistant coaches do a lot of the on-field coaching as far as position coaching goes. That's the way Bud was here at Saint Louis. He would delegate the hands-on coaching out to his assistants, and he would bring the team together as a group in discussing the opponent.

In 1974, 1975, and 1976 we had some really good teams. We won the (NFC East) division, and that was the division that included the Dallas Cowboys and Washington Redskins. We were very close to having a great team. That was the frustration that Coryell had and then Bud had. They weren't able to have the input they wanted to get the few players that we needed to fill some spots. They didn't have any influence really in who the Cardinals drafted or in which players we kept from becoming free agents. In a situation like that, you're never sure who has final say in player-personnel decisions.

Look at a team in the present like the Rams. They seem to have a very good organization as far as having people who can evaluate the talent and the draft, as well as those who can negotiate the contracts. They have a good handle on being able to keep the players they want to keep and how to decide which players to make available to other teams. They've been able to build a really nice team there in Saint Louis, something which we had been close to doing in the mid-seventies. But we were never able to get over the top, which goes to show the importance of being able to keep a head coach and the front office on the same page for a period of years so that you can build something.

I played fourteen years for the Cardinals and always love it when they win, even after they left Saint Louis. I don't follow them that closely now, so I really don't know their personnel all that well. They made a really nice run in the playoffs about five years ago, but just haven't been able to sustain it.

⚭⚭⚭

Jim Hanifan:

A lot of guys would have been intimidated by the players or the staff and wouldn't want it to be known that they were having to learn the game. Not Bud. He came right out and told the players. He said, "Okay, look, guys, I've been out of the game for fourteen years, so as these assistant coaches are talking and explaining things to you, I will also be listening and learning. So we're all in this together."

He didn't try to BS his way through this. Bud said, "What I'm going to try to do is manage all this, and try to do the best that I can to create the best environment I can for you fellas." One thing a player can do, just like a little kid, is pick out a phony. And Bud was no phony.

⚬⚏⚬

In the four seasons preceding Wilkinson's arrival, Coryell's Cardinals had posted records of 10-4, 11-3, 10-4, and 7-7, with the latter including losses in the last four games of the season. Even though the Cardinals didn't get past the first round in either of the two years they made the playoffs during that stretch (1974 and 1975), they probably were only a player or two away from having a Super Bowl-caliber team. **Roger Wehrli** *explains:*

We needed to strengthen our defense a little bit more. We had a good solid defense, but not a great defense. Offensively, we had a great line through those years. Hart was one of the best quarterbacks in the league, a very steady guy who was an excellent passer. Jim was a lot like what Kurt Warner is today for the Rams—a guy who really had a knack for hitting his receivers when they were in full stride.

It was a situation where we had a lot of good players, but we seemed to waste a lot of draft choices through the mid-seventies, drafting players who didn't really help our team. It became an attrition thing, which not only was a problem with some key players but also something that would give any head (coach) doubts about wanting to stick it out. Coryell was a great coach and just didn't feel he was getting the support he needed to do the things that he wanted to do. So he left and went out to San Diego, where he turned them into a very good team with guys like (quarterback) Dan Fouts.

⟨≈⟩

Dan Dierdorf *played right tackle as a mainstay on the Cardinals'* *exceptional offensive line:*

In those days the Cardinal coach had no input into the draft at all. George Boone (the Cardinals' director of player personnel at the time) ran the draft, and that was just the way it was. Don Coryell knew he had a potent offensive team, and if we were ever going to get over the hump, it had to be by improving the defense. . . . Unbelievably, on draft day in 1977, George Boone selects Steve Pisarkiewicz, the quarterback. . . . With Jim Hart in the prime of his career, they draft Steve. Don Coryell went up like a bottle rocket. It was the beginning of the end of the Coryell regime. That's the way it was when Bud was there, too.[1]

⟨≈⟩

Roger Wehrli:

When a coach doesn't have the ability to do what he wants to do and doesn't have the ability to start who he wants to start, it's tough to build a winner. That has been a problem with the Cardinals for a long time. That's what caused Coryell to leave and Bud to get fired. What can you say? I don't even remember how I found out that Bud had been fired. Those things kind of blow your mind when they happen. Bud was such a class individual. Even after he got fired, he and his wife stayed here in the Saint Louis area and remained very involved in charities and other civic activities. And Bud would never say anything bad about (his firing).

⟨≈⟩

Bud Wilkinson, in his early sixties, happy to be back in coaching, this time with the Cardinals.

PHOTOGRAPH COURTESY OF ARIZONA CARDINALS

*The way **Jim Otis** saw it, Wilkinson figured he would be able to work through the ball and chain to eventually build a winning team. All he needed was time:*

I think Bud thought he could have a relationship with the owner that was different from his predecessors, but he could just never do that. That was his ultimate demise with the Cardinals because Mr. Bidwill was going to run it his way, which was the same way he had been running. He wasn't going to let Bud Wilkinson or anyone else come in and change that.

Bud never really had a chance in the pros. He really didn't have the time. I think he was hired in March, which is pretty late in the year to take over a new head coaching position, putting you a month or two behind other coaches in getting ready for the next season. That included being able to put together a staff.

183

Here was a guy of high intellect and great organizational skills, but he couldn't use those things with the Cardinals because that's not what they wanted in a coach. He needed time to get his feet on the ground and to find out what the National Football League was really all about. Bud had a lot to give, even though some of my teammates didn't quite feel the same way, that he was a fish out of water. Everybody can believe what they want to believe, but given more time Bud would have been successful because he had such a great track record of success. He tried.

Some people had the wrong impression of Bud. He was the ultimate kind of guy who wore the velvet slippers: When he was standing on your toe, you might not know it at the time, but you'll find out later. Bud was a guy who meant what he said. But because he was such a gentleman and first-class individual, some people mistook that.

❧

*After the Cardinals finished Wilkinson's first season there at 6-10, the coach started to make some personnel moves as part of a youth movement that meant the rebuilding process was well under way. One of the moves meant Wilkinson telling **Otis** that his services were no longer needed. How Wilkinson handled Otis's situation convinced the veteran of the coach's compassion:*

The next year Bud came to me and wanted me to retire. I don't know if Bud otherwise would have cut me or what he would have done, but after the 1978 season he said to me, "Jim, I'm bringing these young kids in and we have to rebuild, and we have to play these people. You've had a great career, and I just don't want to see you watching and biding your time. You're a player and you need to be playing, and we're going to go in a different direction with younger kids."

So I decided to retire. And even though it was a tough thing, he had me over to his home that evening for dinner to discuss all this, to include my future. What other coach do you know who would ever have done that? He was a special sort of guy.

I played for some great coaches—Woody Hayes, Hank Stram, Don Coryell, and Bud Wilkinson. They're all household names in the world of football. They all had one common thread, and that is that they cared deeply about their players and not just because they could make first downs. I played for the best. Every one of them had common threads, but then every one of those guys was quite different from each other. When these guys talked about character, they knew what they were talking about.

<hr>

Jim Hart:

As far as coaching, I really enjoyed his style. He wasn't what you would call a hard guy. He didn't cuss, for one thing, and he treated you like a man. I appreciated him, but very few of us did. Some players didn't allow themselves to get to know him.

He became a father figure to me, because we spent a lot of time together, on the field and off the field. But maybe that was just the quarterback-coach relationship that exists in most situations. I would hear guys talking about him and would tell them, "Hey, you just need to get to know him," and they really didn't appear to want to. That's too bad. I feel guilty that I didn't get to know him better, although we remained friends and stayed in touch over the years until his death.

He forgot more football than I ever knew. He tried to be innovative, but his innovations didn't work for us because there was a lack of talent. And I don't think he was trying to be innovative just to combat the media's portrayal of him as a coach left behind by the game. Bud wasn't like that. We did some things offensively that media and some players scoffed at, saying, "See, the game really has passed you by." Like the full-house backfield we would employ every once in a while, which we had done sometimes under Coryell in goal line or short-yardage situations. With the full-house backfield, you could go in any direction, and the defense would have trouble recognizing your weak side.

⚬━━━⚬

If there was a high point in Wilkinson's twenty-nine-game tenure with the Cardinals, it was their winning six of their last eight games of the 1978 season. This was after starting the season, Wilkinson's first there, with eight straight losses. **Jim Otis**:

I wouldn't call winning six of our last eight that season as turning a corner. When you take a good look at all the teams in the NFL, you can see that there really isn't that much of a difference in talent level from team to team. What makes a difference is leadership and chemistry—it takes all sorts of things to build a team.

Bud had new things that he wanted to do, and then we had a tragedy in training camp (the 1979 practice-field death of promising tight end J. V. Cain). Bud was like no other coach I ever had. After J. V.'s death, and after J. V.'s parents had picked who they wanted for pallbearers, Bud picked the phone up, and just like that he had three corporate jets for all of us waiting to take us down to Houston for the funeral. We were back that night for practice. Not too many people could have done that, but he wanted to make sure that J. V.'s family had what they needed.

CRITICAL

Jim Hanifan:

Golly, we turned that baby around in 1978 and won six of the last eight games, and those two losses could have gone either way. What a fantastic turnaround that would have been, finishing 8-8! I marveled at Bud's character and his handling of the players and the coaching staff. The man never lost his composure. He never scapegoated a player or a coach. He did a marvelous job.

Being around him seven days a week for almost twenty-four-hour days, I could see this guy in his early sixties who was so active and energetic. He must have been a real pistol in his younger days coaching at Oklahoma. The guy was awesome.

When we beat the Philadelphia Eagles to finally win our first game in that 1978 season, Bud's first with the Cardinals, everyone was just euphoric. It was like we had won the Super Bowl. Bud had tears in his eyes, and I couldn't help but think how neat that was for him.

CRITICAL

Hanifan:

Bud had a way with people; he had a great relationship with the media, and he was able to handle the pressure. He would always be thinking about what sort of motivational talk he could give to the team to really make them think.

One thing he liked to do was to recite poems. With each poem, he would find what the central theme was, and then relate it to whatever our upcoming task was. But Bud had good intentions, and he really knew what he was talking about.

Bud strikes a friendly pose upon being named coach of the Cardinals, secure in the knowledge that he wouldn't have to play quarterback himself—he already had a veteran quarterback in Jim Hart.

PHOTOGRAPH COURTESY OF ARIZONA CARDINALS

One night we had a party up at his place, and I think I might have been the last one to leave the party that night. I figured it was as good a time as any to tell the boss what I was thinking. I said, "Coach, I need to tell you something. You know how you recite these poems to the fellows? You recite a poem by Robert Frost and most of these guys are going, 'Who in the hell is Robert Frost? Doesn't he play for the New York Jets?' Coach, you have, maybe, five college graduates in the whole group, and hardly any of the rest of them even took one English literature course. You know what you need to do, Coach? You need to really fire these guys up and throw a few 'damns' and 'hells' into these talks, things like that."

"Do you really think so?" he said. "Yeah, I think you ought to at least try it." Bud could swear like the rest of us, it's just that you hardly ever heard him do it.

188

After having this discussion with Bud, I went and told the other guys that they could really look forward to the next Saturday night pregame speech, that Bud would have something totally different prepared, that he was really going to jump on the guys and fire them up. Come the next Saturday night, though, and Bud starts right off reciting another poem, this one by Alfred Tennyson, I think. The guys got a chuckle out of that, not at Bud's expense, but in homage to the fact that this was a guy who stuck with his convictions and believed strongly in the way he was doing things.

❧

One of the offensive innovations Wilkinson was working on with the Cardinals was a full-house backfield that would include the tight end. **Jim Hart**:

We would put the tight end in motion one way or the other, and it made the defense declare what was strong and what was weak. That was good from our standpoint, but then (tight end) J. V. Cain died on the practice field before the 1979 season. He was going to be a star, and he was perfect for that role.

We didn't have a backup who had the talent that J. V. did. Jackie Smith, a former tight end of ours, was available, just five miles away, but Bill wouldn't let Bud bring Jackie back to the team to play the tight end position for us. Instead, Jackie ended up going to the Dallas Cowboys and playing in the Super Bowl.

J. V.'s death really cast a shadow over the team. He was going to be the All-Pro that Jackie Smith was. There's no question about that because he worked so hard and was very talented. His death was the precursor of what would be a dismal year. We never recovered from it.

❧

Cain's untimely death during training camp was the first big domino to fall in 1979, sending the Cardinals reeling to a 3-10 start, with six of the losses being by a margin of six points or fewer. No matter, Wilkinson had run out of time. Hart discusses the firing:

I remember it vividly. (General Manager) Larry Wilson replaced Bud for the rest of the season. Bidwill had told Bud that perhaps it was time to see what Steve Pisarkiewicz, who was my backup at quarterback, could do. Bud said that was ridiculous—he was trying to be nice—but then Bill told him no, that he wanted to see what Steve could do. Bud said, "I can tell you what he can do—nothing." Bill insisted that he needed to find out if he could play. Bud kept saying, "I'm telling you, he's not a player." And Bill said that we had nothing to lose and that we should go ahead and at least give it a try.

So Bud puts Steve in in place of me and we end up beating the 49ers, 13-10. Bud said afterward, "That probably makes Bidwill happy." I think that was one of the two times that I ever heard Bill Bidwill address the team. It's usually when he was replacing the coach that he talked to us as a group. In the locker room after the game, he came over and made a snide remark to me: "I'll have you know that your coach wants you traded." I said, "Oh, really? You know, Bill, Bud and I are really close friends, and I'll find out from him if that's the case or not. I think that's very mean-spirited on your part, and I don't believe what you are saying."

I talked to Bud later on that day. And I told him, "Bidwill said a nasty thing to me today. He said that you wanted me traded." Bud said: "That's not exactly what I said. Let me tell you what I said. When all this stuff came down about having to play Pisarkiewicz, I finally said, 'You know, Bill, if you're not going to play Hart, let him go someplace where he can play, someplace where he's wanted.' Bill told me that wasn't going to happen. I told him, 'I want to be coach, and I want Jim Hart to be my quarterback. But if he's not going to play, trade him.'" I said, "Bud, that sounds like you." And he said, "That's exactly what I said." I never said anything about that to Bidwill again.

⌀〰〰〰⌀

There might have been more to Wilkinson's firing, however, than just wins, losses, and the playing status of Steve Pisarkiewicz. **Hart** *explains:*

Part of Bud's demise was that he worked really hard that year trying to put together a consortium of people, and we players knew that Bud knew some people who were really well connected. Bud would tell us weekly, if not daily, "Hang in there, guys. You shouldn't have to put up with this bull. If I can get all my ducks in a row, we're going to end up owning the team and it'll be a good situation for you." We kind of looked at each other and said, "Ooooooo. He probably shouldn't be making that public," and sure enough, that probably had as much to do as anything with his not going on anymore as coach.

Getting back to the quarterback situation, Bidwill asked Bud if he was going to play Pisarkiewicz and Bud said no, that he wouldn't do it. And Bill apparently said, "Then I'll get somebody who will." Bud said, "That's fine, but I'm not going to do it. It's silly and it's not in the best interests of the team." Funny thing, though, is that the team won two of the next three games that we played after Bud's firing. We beat the 49ers and the Giants, and then went into Chicago, and that was a bad experience for Steve. It was a brutally cold day, and he couldn't do it.

The score was 21-0 at halftime, and I was freezing. Soldier Field is a bad place to be playing when it's cold and windy, being right off Lake Michigan. We get into the locker room at halftime, and teammates are saying to me, "You know they're going to be coming at you to ask you to play." I said, "Nah, they wouldn't do that." And they said, "Yeah. You watch." By this time, I had my shoes and socks off and was rubbing my feet because I was frozen. I had my head down the whole time as different people walked by, and all of a sudden here's a team official standing in front of me and saying, "Well, pardner, you probably know why I'm here."

"Yeah, probably."

"The man (Larry Wilson, the interim coach) asked me to come ask you if you would play."

"Oh, he did, did he? He didn't have the guts to come ask me himself, huh?"

"Nope."

"What happened?"

"First, what's your answer? You want me to go back and tell him no?"

"Not particularly."

"Does that mean you're saying yes?"

"No, not particularly . . . but I guess I'll go."

So I went out and started the second half and we went right down the field and scored a touchdown, boom, right off the first series. But on the touchdown pass, the Bears sent an all-out blitz and I got knocked out. I think it was Doug Plank who got me on a safety blitz. I read it perfectly and so did Pat Tilley, and I got the ball into Pat's hands for the touchdown. But as I threw it, I kind of left my feet on a jump-pass type of thing, and Plank drilled me in the chest, and I hit the back of my head on the turf. I was out cold. So Steve went back in because I was unable to continue.

Now I was worse off. Again, there I was sitting out on the cold sidelines, this time not being able to move at all and freezing my butt off.

Later after that game, a bunch of players met for a Christmas party back in Saint Louis and presented him with this big collage of players' and coaches' faces, with Bud's in the middle, that had been created by a really good caricaturist from the *Saint Louis Post-Dispatch* I had commissioned. It's really neat. We had a ball in presenting that to him, even though only about a third of the guys contributed to it. But that's just the way a lot of players were—they would have done that with any coach. It's just how some players are: They'll give you lip service, but when it comes time to ante up, you can't find them. It was a great time that night. It was a very touching moment and a lot of people got choked up over it, Bud included. He was an emotional guy and didn't have any problems when it came to shedding a tear.

❧

Jim Hanifan, who had been Wilkinson's offensive-line coach in 1978, left after that season to join Don Coryell's staff in San Diego. Hanifan's departure was short-lived: After Wilkinson was let go and the Cardinals had finished 4-12, Bidwill went out and hired Hanifan back to be head coach. **Hanifan***:*

After I took the position, one of the first phone calls I got when I arrived in Saint Louis came from Bud. This might have been my second day back in town. I told him, "Hey, Bud, I really appreciate the call, and I'm so sorry how things worked out for you there." He said, "Hey, Jim, don't worry about it. That's the way these things are in football. I just want to wish you the very best of success." That just meant a great deal to me. What a classy guy. Class oozed from every pore in that guy's body.

❦

Roger Wehrli:

The thing about Bud that I remembered the most were the great stories that he would tell and weave into a motivational speech the night before a game. We stayed in a hotel the night before a game, whether it was an away game or a home game, and we always had that team meeting that night before. He would always have this terrific story about one of his Oklahoma teams or a particular individual he had coached. Those were really great moments, and he was able to make it work without sounding just like some guy reminiscing about the past with no real purpose.

❦

Jim Otis:

Bud Wilkinson was the sort of guy who could walk into the locker room and tell his guys what he wanted them to do, and that night he could be sitting with the corporate captains of Saint Louis. He could go from crowd to crowd and make everybody feel important. He would make people feel good by his graciousness.

BUD'S LEGACY

Regardless of the extent to which the Saint Louis experience had tarnished Wilkinson's coaching record, those who knew him continued to hold Wilkinson in the highest regard well after his death in January 1994.

Former Oklahoma quarterback **David Baker**:

His legacy was such that the guy in a small-town barbershop in Oklahoma could feel special about being an Oklahoman, such as when Oklahoma beat Notre Dame or whatever.

After the dust storms of the thirties and early forties, Oklahoma didn't have a really good public image across the country. But the success of Oklahoma football had a lot to do with changing that image for the better. And that wasn't just for the uneducated guy sitting in some barbershop some-where—it was for the guy sitting up in the Petroleum Club, too.

It made them feel pretty special, and that helps explain why Coach Wilkinson was able to travel in all kinds of circles.

The people of Oklahoma, just like the people of Nebraska later, felt special because of the way their football team played. It might have been even more special then, back in the late forties and through the fifties, because in those days you didn't separate football from the rest of society as you do now—they were interwoven, almost intimately.

❦

Eddie Crowder, another of Wilkinson's quarterbacks:

Having known and coached against the likes of Bear Bryant, Woody Hayes, and Bob Devaney, I always thought there was one discernible difference between the great legends that made Bud stand alone. I felt he was the greatest master psychologist of the game. When you're winning forty-seven games in a row—and, granted, you're playing a few teams each year that aren't very good, and yet a few that are very good—you had your football team really ready to play forty-seven times in a row.

My observation would be when arguing about the greatest coach of all time, that here's a guy whose teams won forty-seven in a row not long after they had won thirty-one in a row. That's a nearly "back-to-back" feat that no other coach or school in history has ever even come really close to matching or beating. That's all the evidence you need. To win that many games in a row, there is very little room for error and very little room for a letdown.

Getting a team ready to play a nationally ranked or a really challenging opponent is a monumental task. The brilliance in coaching comes when you get a team really ready to play an

Wilkinson being honored at a banquet in Oklahoma, several years before he passed away.

OKLAHOMA UNIVERSITY FOOTBALL MEDIA RELATIONS OFFICE

inferior opponent. As a coach in those instances, you've got to get your team going out on the field thinking, *Omigosh, we could lose this thing.* The kind of mental conditioning for either of those types of games has to start no later than Tuesday of that week. Bud had a great ability to manage that, to keep his teams from suffering any sort of letdown.

෴

Jay Wilkinson, one of Bud's two sons, went on to an All-American stint playing for Duke in the early sixties. Less than a year after his father's death in 1994, Jay Wilkinson authored a book on his dad, Bud Wilkinson: An Intimate Portrait of an American Legend, *in which he paid his respects to the father he loved:*

197

Not every person handles fame—or life—as graciously as Dad did. As his vigor waned in recent years, and I saw him coping with some of the exigencies poor health can bring, I was struck by the fact that his warmth and dignity never deserted him, even in his last days.

I began to wonder what the source of his great personal power was. What had made him such a success in so many areas of endeavor? I think Dad was a unique combination of good genes and a sound environment. Clearly his upbringing provided a basic moral framework on which he built his entire life, but he was a highly sensitive, talented person from the moment he first made his appearance in the family.[1]

○━━━○

Jim Hanifan, one of Bud's coaching assistants at Saint Louis and, later, Wilkinson's successor as Cardinals head coach, remembers Wilkinson for an important lesson in life he gave him several years after Bud had been fired from the Cardinals:

I can remember after I got fired myself after six seasons there: Like anybody else, I had people calling me, offering me new positions. Some were in radio or television. One guy offered me a position heading up four or five of his hotels.

What really helped me at this time was a statement that Bud had once made to me. He, along with one of his sons (Jay Wilkinson), had an insurance program that ran plans for corporations. Bud told me a story that I never forgot: "We had just won a big contract for securing a pension program with some big, well-known organization, and it meant a heckuva lot of money for us. We had a big party to celebrate. We had gotten the champagne, hors d'oeuvres and all that, and everyone was just elated and having a wonderful time. I was standing amid all this thinking, I should be the happiest guy here because it means more money in my pocket than anybody's. But I had this horrible feeling: This is it? This is it? I had no feeling, and it dawned on me that this was nothing compared to going into South Bend, Indiana, with my Oklahoma team and beating Notre Dame. When I hit that locker room, now that was something special. Jim, I want you to remember this, because the day will come when you will be offered a job like this, and I want you to be very, very careful about it."

That really kept me in the game. And, golly, he was right.

ⓒⓘⓘⓘⓘ৯

*As much as **David Baker** admired the Great White Father while playing at Oklahoma, his appreciation for Wilkinson and the way he did things at Oklahoma really hit him once he got to the NFL after being drafted in the first round by the San Francisco 49ers in 1959:*

Oklahoma football under Coach Wilkinson and the NFL were two totally different things. I can remember when they had the College All-Star Game against the NFL, and playing with the college all-stars when I was a rookie with the San Francisco 49ers. I flew back the next day, a Sunday, and had to get ready for an exhibition game later that day. It was my first exhibition game and I can still remember going into the 49ers locker room on a game day for the first time.

I remembered back to when I was playing at Oklahoma and how when it was game day, no one said a word in the locker room unless it was the coaches. Not a word. We were supposed to be concentrating on the game. There was no place for a guy to be talking to his buddy about what movie they were going to go see that night.

Then I get to the 49ers, and it was like a circus in there.
That's how it appeared to me. Guys were bouncing off the walls,
smoking cigarettes, bumming cigarettes from the coaches . . .
stuff like that. It was just unreal. Screaming and hollering. The
biggest difference was the mental attitude you would have in
preparing for the game. I eventually found out from some other
players in the pros that this was no different from their locker-
room experiences back in college, and this included guys who
had played at Michigan State under Duffy Daugherty. I know
Coach Wilkinson and Coach Daugherty were good friends, but
they were total opposites from each other in personality.

∞∞∞

Veteran television college football announcer **Keith Jackson**
*weighs in with this assessment of Wilkinson's place in history among
the game's greatest coaches:*

I know that Paul "Bear" Bryant has long since been accorded
the title of being "the greatest football rules changer of all
time," which is something that rules guru David Nelson out of
Delaware said. Bud has some impact as well, but not to the
degree that Paul did. Bud was doing some very subtle little
things that would upset the opposition, but by the time they
recovered their equilibrium he normally had them licked.

Above all that, Bud understood what Amos Alonzo Stagg
once said about how "big, fast people usually beat little, fast
people." Bud assembled big numbers of people and he put
speed at a lot of unusual positions. His defensive ends were
men of exceptional speed; not, perhaps, as swift as they are
today, but nonetheless in his time he had more speed at the
defensive end and linebacking positions than anybody else
had. And he would put some of his best athletes at the

cornerback positions so that people wouldn't be able to throw the ball against him.

He was a great believer in foot speed and he was an exceptional salesman, as the world knows. I think the only contest he tried to win and didn't was the U.S. Senate. Golfer Patty Berg once said that he learned all of that from her. They grew up playing street football together in Minneapolis.

⊙⚏⚏⚏⚏⚏⚏⚏⚏⚏⚏◐

Jackson can't talk long about Wilkinson without bringing Bear Bryant into the conversation, and vice versa:

Bryant and Wilkinson were two totally different people, or at least the perception of them was totally different, but there were a lot of similarities between them, too.

The best locker room speech that Paul ever gave was before a Tennessee game. He walked into the locker room, lit a Chesterfield, and walked around and looked at each of these kids sweatin' bullets. He started to wonder if half of them were going to faint before they kicked off. So he smoked and he walked and he talked, mainly mumbling to himself. Finally he got to the door, turned back to them, and said, "Boys, I know you're prepared. I know you believe in yourself. So all you have to do is be brave." And he walked out, and they ended up beating one of the great Tennessee teams, which had come to town undefeated.

⊙⚏⚏⚏⚏⚏⚏⚏⚏⚏⚏◐

Chris Schenkel, like Jackson, worked a number of years as ABC's play-by-play man whose duties included "handing off" to Wilkinson dozens of times during the course of calling a game:

Bud had a wonderful sense of values—all kinds of values. I think they probably came from the way he grew up. He had a lot of admiration for the people who surrounded him. He talked about his family all the time. And he had a lot of compassion. My God, he'd see a wounded bird in the form of a person—a wounded sparrow I call them—and he'd stop and talk to them and never look down on them. I never saw him look down on anyone.[2]

ᏆᎥᎥᎥᎥᎥᎥᎥᎥᎥᎥᎥᎥᎥ

Veteran network television sportscaster **John Derr** *remembers a chance meeting with Wilkinson:*

In 1952 *Look* magazine selected twenty-two All-American college football stars—a squad of eleven defensive players and a like number of offensive players. *Look* brought the oversized squad and some of the more visible coaches to New York for an awards dinner at Momma Leone's restaurant, the deservedly favorite eating emporium on West Forty-eighth Street.

To tell the world about the accomplishments of these muscular mastodons of mayhem, CBS Radio was chosen to broadcast the event. Red Barber, CBS Sports chieftain and the best interviewer in the business, realized he would not be able to elicit the human interest stories from so many in so few minutes.

"You will get a chance to do some interviews," Barber revealed when we arrived at the crowded restaurant, which had been closed that night from the public.

Our CBS engineer had set up his equipment in a room that would not be used this stag evening. I went ahead to check out the mike and Barber brought in my first guest, Bud Wilkinson. We shook hands and got under way.

Thereafter, when anyone asked if in my career I had ever met Bud Wilkinson, a lot of surprised eyebrows were lifted

Bud was a man of few words and perhaps even somewhat shy, but when he spoke, he spoke from the heart and people listened.

when I replied, "Oh, yes. I met Coach Wilkinson at Leone's Restaurant . . . in the ladies' room."

❧

Terry Jastrow was one of many television sports people whose career foundation was built largely on their involvement with ABC's coverage of college football:

He was so polite and such a gentleman to everyone. There was absolutely no reason he should have taken the time and care to look an eighteen-year-old college kid like me in the eye and be gracious and warm and polite. But he was. He made you feel like you were important and you mattered to him. You figured he'd do it with Roone Arledge and Chris (Schenkel) and Darrell Royal, but he treated everybody the same.[3]

ᏆᎥᎥᎥᎥᎥᎥᎥᎥᎩ

Many college football experts, when comparing great coaches of the Wilkinson era, will most often refer to the likes of Woody Hayes and Bear Bryant. Often overlooked is legendary Army coach Red Blaik, whose many coaching protégés over the years included one Vince Lombardi. **Ara Parseghian** *talks about Blaik and Bud in practically the same breath:*

Red Blaik was a very reserved, almost stoic-like personality. He wasn't an effervescent, outgoing person. He had the calmness but not the personality, smile, and communication ability that Bud had. Blaik, with a military background, walking into a room he was a similar personality in how he commanded attention. Even though Bud was a low-key guy, he was a more personable guy and therefore easier to communicate with. He came along at the right time with the right system, the right plan, and the right staff. He was able to do a lot of things right to be able to run up the kind of consecutive game-winning streaks that he had. That speaks volumes about what he was able to do.

ᏆᎥᎥᎥᎥᎥᎥᎥᎥᎩ

Jim Hart, *Wilkinson's starting quarterback during his one-plus seasons with the Cardinals, finds it ironic how Wilkinson's failed attempt to add innovation to the offense with a tight end in a full-house backfield was later successful elsewhere:*

Interestingly enough, four or five years later, Sam Wyche, an NFL coach, came up with this idea of putting a tight end in the backfield and moving him in motion, and all of a sudden, everybody's saying, "Wow! Look at this innovation! Isn't he smart?"

I'd read about this in the paper or heard about it during a tele-cast and I'd think, You dumb cluck. Bud Wilkinson was doing this four or five years ago and you said the game had passed him by—What's the story here? A young guy comes up with it, and suddenly it's innovative.

ೲೲ

Bobby Bowden, *the longtime Florida State coach, on attending a Coach of the Year clinic that featured Bud in 1955:*

He lectured on the option. That was kind of a new offense back then. I just salivated. I'll never forget—Bud demon-strated how the quarterback ran the option as I sat in the stands with the other high school and college coaches. That will always be one of my great memories. And I've told my coaches quite a few times about how he said, "I don't coach X's and O's: I coach people."[4]

ೲೲ

Eddie Crowder *quotes Scripture in paying a final tribute to Wilkinson:*

> Love is patient, love is kind. It does not envy, it does not
> boast, it is not proud. It is not rude, it is not self-seeking,
> it is not easily angered, it keeps no record of wrongs.
> Love does not delight in evil but rejoices with the truth. It
> always protects, always trusts, always hopes, always per-
> severes. Love never fails.

—1 Corinthians 13:4-8
New International Version

As I have sought to absorb all that over the years, it has continually occurred to me that Bud lived by all of them. And he was the only person I've known who did. When you are coaching a highly visible college football team and can live by the standards of this kind in all your behavior, you are rare and unique. He was.

⚮

Patty Berg, an LPGA Hall of Famer who grew up in Minnesota with Wilkinson, even playing youth football with him:

He had all the characteristics of a champion. You could tell that because he was always captain of our team. . . . A lot of people have the wish to win, but champions have the will to win. That's what Bud had. He always strived for perfection. He was a good athlete, but more than that, too. He was a great leader. . . . He could take a mediocre team and make them champions. . . . He knew how to treat his boys to get the best out of them, and he knew how to have them play football to have fun, which is what a student ought to do.[5]

In His Own Words

Wilkinson spoke softly but he carried a big vocabulary. He didn't have to raise his voice to be heard, loud and clear.

***

Alumni

The average alumnus looks at the scoreboard and sees that one team won and the other lost—so the team that won was smartly coached, well conditioned, ran the proper offense, used the right defenses, and had outstanding morale. The other team was stupid. That's about the way most of them look at it.[1]

***

Boredom

Paperwork bores me. I hate monotony of any kind.[2]

⚭

Brainpower

The fact our men believe they can use their brains to defeat a physically superior opponent pays dividends you can't reckon with—they're so great.[3]

⚭

The Cardinals

I didn't anticipate coaching again when I left Oklahoma. The fact the Cardinals opportunity occurred really came out of the blue without any prior planning on my part. I thought it would be fun to do and it was.[4]

I know the power that exists on the side of management. The fine system is in place, and if somebody chooses to become very technically legal about it, it could cost the players a lot of money to do those things. I didn't feel it was going to make any difference in what the final result would be.[5] (*Addressing a threat by Cardinals players to boycott after learning that Wilkinson had been fired as head coach*)

The only disappointment I had was that when I joined the Cardinals the offensive line was the pride of the team. They were awfully good. I think they allowed the least sacks in the league the year before, and the year before that. They were very big people. But the pros have this myth that every step you make them take in practice is a step off their careers.[6]

⚭

Wilkinson was a nut for physical fitness long before it was fashionable.

Character

Character is the foundation on which the program must be built. A steadfast devotion to honesty, a positive climate of fairness, and a constant respect for individual human dignity must exist at all times.

∞

Coaching

This (coaching the Saint Louis Cardinals) was no different from any other coaching job I've had. Coaching is the same whether you're talking about high school or college or professional football.[7]

One thing I learned long ago about coaching is that you have to be yourself. The demands are too great for too long a period of time to maintain any kind of act.[8]

⧼⧽

The College Game

The college coach must adjust his tactics not just to the talent available, but to the talent available that particular season. Because of the rapid turnover in personnel, every season is a new battle, calling for a new strategy—which had better be right.[9]

⧼⧽

Competitiveness

If you're out there just to take up space, you aren't playing the game. It's meant to be played as well as you can play. If you're just joking around, you aren't doing credit to yourself or the game.[10]

⧼⧽

Conditioning

When you're in a game, you may play twelve minutes or forty-six minutes, but somewhere the dike begins to crack. If a player hasn't conditioned himself previously, he'll probably not have the fortitude or courage—football won't mean enough to him—to recover a punt when he's tired and it's ninety-six degrees on the playing field. "There are eleven fights out there," I tell my men, "we've got to win seven of them."[11]

⚬⚬⚬

Defense

Offense is easy, but it takes a man to play defense!

If we keep the other fellow from scoring, we'll never lose a football game.

⚬⚬⚬

Education

Education in the final analysis is simply the development of self-discipline of the mind. James Conant, former president of Harvard, once said, "Your education is what you have left over when you have forgotten all that you have learned."

If you can bear down on your studies and do well in them, even though you do not have a great deal of interest in them, think how simple and easy it will be to do well when you are highly motivated and truly enjoy the work.[12] *(In a letter to his son Jay, who at the time was having academic difficulties at Duke)*

⚬⚬⚬

Emotion

If you've ever been around an athletic team in any sport, you understand the human relationships that evolve; the intensity of the experience, the fascination with the game itself. The heights of joy are acute, the depths of depression are acute. There is nothing quite like it.[13]

◇━━◇

Enthusiasm

Enthusiasm is the whole point of college football.[14]

◇━━◇

Excellence

The achievement of excellence is important. However, sportsmanship must never give way to unfair practices in order to win games. Excellence of performance and sportsmanship are not incompatible—in fact, the very opposite is true. Proper mental and physical habits, self-discipline, and intelligent practice are essential in order to achieve excellence in any sport.

◇━━◇

Faith

As I see it, there has to be something more to life than just day-to-day living. Otherwise, there would be little incentive for decency and honesty. The church best exemplifies the better things of this life. And the church is certainly the greatest moral force in our country.[15]

◇━━◇

Fans

The fans have come to expect a good performance, and the boys aren't going to let them down.[16]

৩্যা৩

Football

Football really is crazy. It's for the birds. We're going to move to Minneapolis and live happily ever after.[17] (*In a letter to Mary, written during his days as an officer serving in World War II*)

This is the best brief analysis of football. It isn't winning or losing that has lasting value or importance. The effort, dedication, and sacrifice you make for a cause—your team—the working with others toward a common, most demanding goal (is what matters). The loyalty, the joys, the disappointments, and, above all, learning to give your best mentally, emotionally, and physically are the qualities that make a man, and there is no other place they are learned so well.[18]

Football is a game of speed and movement.

৩্যা৩

Heroes

There aren't enough heroic positions on a football team to have people play because they want to be a hero.[19]

৩্যা৩

Interaction

I think it's psychologically dangerous for kids, and adults, too, to come home and turn on the TV and never read or play cards or talk. They don't try to participate.[20]

CRULO

Killer Instinct

Great football players have the so-called "killer instinct." They don't know how to loaf or ease off on blocks and tackles. They hit as hard as they can and move as fast as they can on every play in both practice and games. This is what makes them great.

CRULO

Leadership

I don't object to people who do not want to do it my way. I just tell them I will make it possible for them to do it their way somewhere else.[21]

CRULO

Losing

The quickest way to lose a football game is by a long breakaway run or a long touchdown pass. If one of our players makes a mistake on the scrimmage line, it only costs us eight yards. But if one of our secondaries makes a mistake, it costs us six points. (*Statement before 1954 season*)

CRULO

Morale

Morale is 90 percent of the game. If you don't have it, you can't win. And if you have it, of course, you need other things to win.[22]

∽≈≈≈≈∾

Motivation

The ideal situation is to have everyone on the squad trying to make the first team at the last practice before the last game.[23]

The coach has one aim and that is to get the best out of each player and to help the player develop in every way. This is what a coach is trying to do with the people who play for him. He first tries to have them understand their potential, and next he presents a challenge to them to be as good as they can be. He hopes this will carry over into other activities in life in which they may become involved. The players' attitude toward you hinges on one thing, and this is respect. If they do not respect you, you have lost them. If you have their respect, you have it made.[24]

The worst thing you can do is underrate an opponent. We always assumed at Oklahoma that we were going to be physically inferior to our opponents. The best we would ever get would be a straight-up draw on talent. That meant that we had to concentrate on ways of winning other than sheer strength or speed.[25]

∽≈≈≈≈∾

Offense

A four-yard gain is a good play. A first down is what we're trying to get, not a touchdown.[26]

∽≈≈≈≈∾

The Pride of Oklahoma Band pays homage to a legendary coach during a halftime ceremony in 1991.

OU FOOTBALL MEDIA RELATIONS OFFICE

Oklahoma

Take two teams that are evenly matched, and, theoretically, each team will have the ball thirty minutes of the game. However, if we run fifteen more plays during our thirty minutes, the yardage we make on those plays is the yardage that will result in victory. We really believed that and taught it and went to great pains to make the players believe it.[27]

Oklahoma never will have as fine a team again. This is the last of the GI groups, and we had a maturity, poise, and experience that we dare not hope for in the future. I know that other coaches were glad to get rid of their GIs, but I never saw a finer group of boys. Their outstanding attribute? This sounds cold-blooded, but it isn't: It was their lack of sympathy.[28] *(Discussing his 1949 team that went 11-0 and finished the season ranked nationally, although three national titles would come the Sooners' way over the next seven seasons)*

Frankly, I'm not interested in records. The thing I'm proudest of is the type of boy represented at Oklahoma in football.[29]

Oklahoma, as you probably know, likes to control the ball. We've been running the plays very fast all season. We think it puts a real burden on the defense; that is, to be ready for the plays coming so fast. If we can run plays real fast and move the ball, we figure we're likely to have the ball more than the other team.[30]

❦

One-Platoon Football

Recruiting in one-platoon football was a lot different than recruiting in two-platoon football. In one-platoon, the moral character of the individual is paramount in the recruiting factor. In two-platoon football, you recruit only for the talent that individual has. His character is not particularly important. I don't mean to indict an awful lot of two-platoon football players who are super people. I don't mean in any way to criticize them. But the game would be better, in my view, if it would return to one-platoon football. Your quarterback doesn't want to play defensive halfback. But in one-platoon football, he does have to play defense. And if he's not a damned good defensive player, you're probably not going to win very much.[31]

❦

Physical Fitness

I just don't believe that you're going to run in place in your bedroom every morning for the rest of your life. Before you get into shape, you'll collapse from boredom.[32]

Physical education has been dominated too long by varsity athletics. The aim has not been to develop physical skills that could be used after a student left school. The aim has been to develop skills that could win games for the varsity teams. That emphasis is all wrong. I'm for varsity athletics, but I'm also a strong supporter of quality physical education programs for every boy and girl.[33] (*Spoken three years after his last season coaching at Oklahoma, while director of the Lifetime Sports Foundation in Washington, D.C.*)

I consider health education a related part of physical education, though some educators separate them. Physical fitness rests on a tripod. That tripod includes adequate rest, a balanced diet, and exercise. Generally, physical education programs are concerned only with exercise.[34]

If a visitor from another planet came to this country and leafed through a few of our magazines, he'd decide that the main goal of our society was to retire as soon as possible and do nothing. I don't believe that's any way to lead a life. When you stop caring how well you do things, you start becoming a vegetable.[35]

We can't fight or run away, as the cavemen did, because we don't do that sort of thing in our society. We stay there and choke it back. And the tensions we build up raise merry hell with our systems because we have no way of releasing them. We men can't even go home and work them off by pushing a lawnmower around the yard. There's a motor on the thing.[36]

Practice

(Ben) Hogan was willing to pay the price in painstaking practice. He was forever trying to reduce the odds against his hitting a bad shot. It's the same in football. Your goal must be high, the very highest. Each player must be giving all he's got. If not, it's like the old business of one rotten apple spoiling the barrel.[37]

⟨∞⟩

Preparation

The things a boy does in August are more important than anything the coaches do after that.[38]

The will to prepare is the key ingredient to success. When the game starts, all the people in the stands and the players hope they will have the will to win. If you lose, all too many times media people and fans say, "The team wasn't ready today. They didn't have the will to win." . . .

The will to prepare is getting out of bed at 5:30 . . . for the morning practice, and you're stiff and sore and you don't want to practice. If you do not practice totally productively, you've wasted that time. That's what I characterize as the will to prepare.[39]

During football season a coach hardly has time to brush his teeth. Four hours of preparation are needed for one hour of practice. If we're going to use our practice to maximum value, we have to know what we're going to do every minute.[40]

People are prone to talk about the will to win. But what makes a winning player special is the will to prepare. When you have that will and dedication to prepare in the days leading up to the game, on game day you have the competence to win.[41]

Games are won by teams that know best how to play football when the game starts. It's not what the coaches know but what the players know.

❦

Quarterbacks

A quarterback who can execute well every technique and skill the position demands is, in my judgment, the most talented of all athletes. This statement may get an argument from decathlon fans or followers of other sports, but I believe the quarterback has the most demanding, difficult assignment in athletics.[42]

I try to teach my quarterbacks everything I know.[43]

❦

Recruiting

You have to recruit young men with athletic ability, but because football is a game of heart and morale, you first have to have a boy of good character who is able to handle college work. He should be able to graduate. If he doesn't have the ability to graduate, he shouldn't be in college.[44]

We recruited only in Oklahoma and the Texas panhandle. I didn't realize that Oklahoma had established a reputation that we maybe could have recruited successfully beyond that little pocket of 150 miles. If I had been smart enough to do that, it might have made our program more successful. My son (Jay) went to Duke, and when he came home, he would say, "Dad, you ought to expand your horizons a little bit." I just didn't ever think we could. But the whole picture has changed today.[45]

You have to remember that the smaller the high school the player comes from and the greater his athletic potential, the more difficulty he will have adjusting to the major college program. He was always so much better than his opponents that he could turn it on whenever he wanted to and dominate the game. Learning to turn it on every play—and having the self-discipline to do it—is a big adjustment. The athlete who comes from a very strong high school league has already learned to do that.[46]

⁓⁓

Retirement

I have no plans to stop coaching. I like coaching very much. Many coaches over fifty are still active, and I'm only forty-six. . . . But, I repeat, I have no plans whatever to stop coaching. (*Spoken eleven months before retiring as Oklahoma coach*)

In moments of reflection, I have often considered this day of retirement from active coaching. I have reached the decision with reluctance. Obviously, I will always owe a debt of gratitude to the players, coaches, faculty, and loyal fans of Oklahoma football who have made these years good beyond anything I deserve. These relationships of mutual trust and respect are the very factors which make it unfair for me to continue coaching at a time when it could be difficult to devote my undivided attention to our team and university. (*An excerpt from Wilkinson's coaching-retirement announcement on January 11, 1964, which was made soon after his brother's death and not long before he formalized his run for the U.S. Senate*)

◯⟁⟁⟁◯

Role Models

Too many adults set bad examples for youth.[47]

◯⟁⟁⟁◯

Smoking

I know all the magazines say to smoke a Camel and hit a home run, but it harms you. If football doesn't mean enough to you to give up smoking, then we're bad off here. If you want to smoke in your own room, we won't object. . . . I hope you won't. Don't smoke in public. Then if we lose, the fans will say we lost because the players didn't train. Football squads with lots of smokers don't play well. No drinking. *(His first speech to his 1955 team before starting August two-a-days)*

◯⟁⟁⟁◯

Split-T Offense

Please don't give me any credit for (devising) the Split-T. It belongs to Don Faurot. I've always felt that he never has received adequate recognition for his contribution to offensive football.[48] *(Faurot was best-known as the head football coach at the University of Missouri.)*

We play the Split-T because we think we can teach it more effectively than any other offense in the short period of practice time allowed us; and the fluid pattern of the play enables our individual linemen to move at will laterally.[49]

Wilkinson shows his appreciation upon being honored during a game at Oklahoma before his death in January 1994.

OKLAHOMA UNIVERSITY FOOTBALL MEDIA RELATIONS OFFICE

CRIMO

Standards

Unless our standards are high in everything, the entire group will retrogress to the lowest level. When we travel, we're going to travel as well as we can. Our uniforms will be the best, and we'll try to look the neatest and be the cleanest and the smartest. In every possible ramification, we're going to try to shoot for the moon. People who are going to play well operate that way. For instance, I don't think a good golfer can play with dirty clubs.[50]

CRIMO

Teaching

There isn't a badly trained team in the country. But there are many coaches who should be better teachers.[51]

If I contributed anything to football of an original nature, it was the Oklahoma 5-2 (defense). We evolved it from the seven-man line, which in that day and time was one of the standard defenses. In order to add a little fluid ability, cover passes, and make adjustments, the 5-2 dropped the ends off the line of scrimmage, so they became linebackers. Now we had five line-men, not seven—two inside linebackers and, now, two outside linebackers. We were able to funnel everything to the middle guard. It was awfully hard to go wide against us.[52]

❧

Texas

I was speaking hypothetically. I sure as hell don't want to leave Oklahoma. Texas, first of all, is a great job. There's no doubt about that. But it was purely accidental that these writers thought I was serious. I certainly don't want to be put in the position of one who is out shopping for another job.[53] *(Denying his reported interest in the vacant University of Texas head coaching job in 1956)*

NOTES

GAME-BY-GAME
COACHING RECORD

INDEX

Notes

Chapter 2: Oklahoma!

1. Jay Wilkinson, with Gretchen Hirsch, *Bud Wilkinson: An Intimate Portrait of an American Legend* (Champaign, Ill.: Sagamore Publishing, 1994), p. 24.
2. Ibid., p. 87.
3. Ibid., pp. 78-79.

Chapter 3: 31; 47; 94-5-2

1. Jim Dent, *The Undefeated* (New York: Thomas Dunne Books, St. Martin's Press, 2001), p. xvi.

Chapter 4: The Great White Father

1. Jay Wilkinson, *Bud Wilkinson*, p. 34.

Chapter 5: The ABC's of Life After Football

1. Jay Wilkinson, *Bud Wilkinson*, p. 130.

2. Ibid., p. 137.

3. Ibid., p. 142.

4. Ibid., p. 172.

5. Ibid., p. 147.

6. Ibid., p. 154.

7. Ibid., pp. 155-56.

8. Ibid., pp. 158-59.

Chapter 6: Playing with the Cards Dealt

1. Jay Wilkinson, *Bud Wilkinson*, p. 216.

Chapter 7: Bud's Legacy

1. Jay Wilkinson, *Bud Wilkinson*, p. 2.

2. Ibid., p. 168.

3. Ibid.

4. Ibid., p. 190.

5. Ibid., p. 3.

Chapter 8: In His Own Words

1. *Sports Illustrated*, circa 1956.

2. Ibid.

3. Ibid.

4. *Oklahoman* and *Times*, May 27, 1980.

5. Ibid.

6. *Scholastic Coach*, May/June 1994.

7. *Daily Oklahoman*, February 25, 1979.

8. Ibid.

9. *Daily Oklahoman*, August 25, 1965.

10. *Sports Illustrated*, circa 1956.

11. Ibid.

12. Jay Wilkinson, *Bud Wilkinson*, p. 103.

13. *Daily Oklahoman*, February 25, 1979.

14. *Life*, November 1956.

15. *Episcopal Churchnews*, February 19, 1956.

16. Associated Press, December 9, 1954.

17. *Daily Oklahoman*, February 11, 1994.

18. Jay Wilkinson, *Bud Wilkinson*, p. 107.

19. *Sports Illustrated*, circa 1956.

20. *Life*, November 1956.

21. *Sooners Illustrated*, March 26, 1994.

22. *Waco News-Tribune*, Augusta 8, 1967.

23. Ibid.

24. Jay Wilkinson, *Bud Wilkinson*, p. 88.

25. Ibid., p. 144.

26. *Life*, November 1956.

27. Jay Wilkinson, *Bud Wilkinson*, p. 31.

28. *New York Times*, sometime after the conclusion of the 1949 season.

29. *Sports Illustrated*, circa 1956.

30. *Episcopal Churchnews*, February 19, 1956.

31. *The Jim and Dee Hunt Edition*, September 29, 1990.

32. Bud Wilkinson, *Bud Wilkinson's Guide to Modern Physical Fitness* (New York: Viking Press, 1967), p. 4.

33. *The Oklahoma Teacher*, February 1966.

34. Ibid.

35. Bud Wilkinson, *Bud Wilkinson's Guide to Modern Physical Fitness*, p. 141.

36. Ibid., p. 8.

37. *Episcopal Churchnews*, February 19, 1956.

38. *Waco News-Tribune*, August 8, 1967.

39. Jay Wilkinson, *Bud Wilkinson*, pp. 28-29.

40. *Sports Illustrated*, circa 1956.

41. Norman Transcript, January 22, 1987.

42. Norman Transcript, September 15, 1965.

43. *Life*, November 1956.

44. Jay Wilkinson, *Bud Wilkinson*, p. 36.

45. *The Jim and Dee Hunt Edition*, September 29, 1990.

46. *Scholastic Coach*, May/June 1994.

47. *Minneapolis Star*, May 5, 1958.

48. *New York Times*, sometime after the conclusion of the 1949 season.

49. *Sports Illustrated*, circa 1956.

50. Ibid.

51. *Life*, November 1956.

52. Jay Wilkinson, *Bud Wilkinson*, p. 33.

53. *Daily Oklahoman*, December 9, 1956.

BUD WILKINSON'S
GAME-BY-GAME COACHING RECORD

Oklahoma Sooners Coaching Record
1947 (7-2-1)
Big Six Champions

Date	Opponent	Site	Result	Score
Sept. 27	Detroit	Away	Win	24-20
Oct. 4	Texas A&M	Home	Win	26-14
Oct. 11	Texas	Dallas	Loss	14-34
Oct. 18	Kansas	Home	Tie	13-13
Oct. 25	Texas Christian	Home	Loss	7-20
Nov. 1	Iowa State	Home	Win	27-9
Nov. 8	Kansas State	Away	Win	27-13
Nov. 15	Missouri	Away	Win	21-12
Nov. 22	Nebraska	Away	Win	14-13
Nov. 29	Oklahoma State	Home	Win	21-13

Final ranking: NR (not ranked)

1948 (10-1)
Big Seven Champions

Date	Opponent	Site	Result	Score
Sept. 25	Santa Clara	Away	Loss	17-20
Oct. 2	Texas A&M	Home	Win	42-14
Oct. 9	Texas	Dallas	Win	20-14
Oct. 16	Kansas State	Home	Win	42-0
Oct. 23	Texas Christian	Away	Win	21-18
Oct. 30	Iowa State	Away	Win	33-6
Nov. 6	Missouri	Home	Win	41-7
Nov. 13	Nebraska	Home	Win	41-14
Nov. 20	Kansas	Away	Win	60-7
Nov. 27	Oklahoma State	Away	Win	19-15

Final ranking: AP, 5th

1949 (11-0)
Big Seven Champions

Date	Opponent	Site	Result	Score
Sept. 23	Boston College	Away	Win	46-0
Oct. 1	Texas A&M	Home	Win	33-13
Oct. 8	Texas	Dallas	Win	20-14
Oct. 15	Kansas	Home	Win	48-26
Oct. 22	Nebraska	Away	Win	48-0
Oct. 29	Iowa State	Home	Win	34-7
Nov. 5	Kansas State	Away	Win	39-0
Nov. 12	Missouri	Away	Win	27-7
Nov. 19	Santa Clara	Home	Win	28-21
Nov. 26	Oklahoma State	Home	Win	41-0

Final ranking: AP, 2nd

1950 (10-1)
Big Seven Champions
National Champions

Date	Opponent	Site	Result	Score
Sept. 30	Boston College	Home	Win	28-0
Oct. 7	Texas A&M	Home	Win	34-28
Oct. 14	Texas	Dallas	Win	14-13
Oct. 21	Kansas State	Home	Win	58-0
Oct. 28	Iowa State	Away	Win	20-7
Nov. 4	Colorado	Away	Win	27-18
Nov. 11	Kansas	Away	Win	33-13
Nov. 18	Missouri	Home	Win	41-7
Nov. 25	Nebraska	Home	Win	49-35
Dec. 2	Oklahoma State	Away	Win	41-14
Jan. 1	Kentucky (Sugar Bowl)		Loss	7-13

Final ranking: AP, 1st; UPI, 1st

1951 (8-2)
Big Seven Champions

Date	Opponent	Site	Result	Score
Sept. 29	William & Mary	Home	Win	49-7
Oct. 6	Texas A&M	Away	Loss	7-14
Oct. 13	Texas	Dallas	Loss	7-9
Oct. 20	Kansas	Home	Win	33-21
Oct. 27	Colorado	Home	Win	55-14
Nov. 3	Kansas State	Away	Win	33-0
Nov. 10	Missouri	Away	Win	34-20
Nov. 17	Iowa State	Home	Win	35-6
Nov. 24	Nebraska	Away	Win	27-0
Dec. 1	Oklahoma State	Home	Win	41-6

Final ranking: AP, 10th; UPI, NR

1952 (8-1-1)
Big Seven Champions

Date	Opponent	Site	Result	Score
Sept. 27	Colorado	Away	Tie	21-21
Oct. 4	Pittsburgh	Home	Win	49-20
Oct. 11	Texas	Dallas	Win	49-20
Oct. 18	Kansas	Away	Win	42-20
Oct. 25	Kansas State	Home	Win	49-6
Nov. 1	Iowa State	Away	Win	41-0
Nov. 8	Notre Dame	Away	Loss	21-27
Nov. 15	Missouri	Home	Win	47-7
Nov. 22	Nebraska	Home	Win	34-13
Nov. 29	Oklahoma State	Away	Win	54-7

Final ranking: AP, 4th; UPI, 4th

1953 (9-1-1)
Big Seven Champions

Date	Opponent	Site	Result	Score
Sept. 26	Notre Dame	Home	Loss	21-28
Oct. 3	Pittsburgh	Away	Tie	7-7
Oct. 10	Texas	Dallas	Win	19-14
Oct. 17	Kansas	Home	Win	45-0
Oct. 24	Colorado	Home	Win	27-20
Oct. 31	Kansas State	Home	Win	34-0
Nov. 7	Missouri	Away	Win	14-0
Nov. 14	Iowa State	Home	Win	47-0
Nov. 21	Nebraska	Away	Win	30-7
Nov. 28	Oklahoma State	Home	Win	42-7
Jan. 1	Maryland (Orange Bowl)		Win	7-0

Final ranking: AP, 4th; UPI, 5th

1954 (10-0)
Big Seven Champions

Date	Opponent	Site	Result	Score
Sept. 18	California	Away	Win	27-13
Sept. 25	Texas Christian	Home	Win	21-16
Oct. 9	Texas	Dallas	Win	14-7
Oct. 16	Kansas	Away	Win	65-0
Oct. 23	Kansas State	Home	Win	21-0
Oct. 30	Colorado	Away	Win	13-6
Nov. 6	Iowa State	Away	Win	40-0
Nov. 13	Missouri	Home	Win	34-13
Nov. 20	Nebraska	Home	Win	55-7
Nov. 27	Oklahoma State	Away	Win	14-0

Final ranking: AP, 3rd; UPI, 3rd

1955 (11-0)
Big Seven Champions
National Champions

Date	Opponent	Site	Result	Score
Sept. 24	North Carolina	Away	Win	13-6
Oct. 1	Pittsburgh	Home	Win	26-14
Oct. 8	Texas	Dallas	Win	20-0
Oct. 15	Kansas	Home	Win	44-6
Oct. 22	Colorado	Home	Win	56-21
Oct. 29	Kansas State	Away	Win	40-7
Nov. 5	Missouri	Away	Win	20-0
Nov. 12	Iowa State	Home	Win	52-0
Nov. 19	Nebraska	Away	Win	41-0
Nov. 26	Oklahoma State	Home	Win	53-0
Jan. 1	Maryland (Orange Bowl)		Win	20-6

Final ranking: AP, 1st; UPI, 1st

1956 (11-0)
Big Seven Champions
National Champions

Date	Opponent	Site	Result	Score
Sept. 29	North Carolina	Home	Win	36-0
Oct. 6	Kansas State	Home	Win	66-0
Oct. 13	Texas	Dallas	Win	45-0
Oct. 20	Kansas	Away	Win	34-12
Oct. 27	Notre Dame	Away	Win	40-0
Nov. 3	Colorado	Away	Win	27-19
Nov. 10	Iowa State	Away	Win	44-0
Nov. 17	Missouri	Home	Win	67-14
Nov. 24	Nebraska	Home	Win	54-6
Dec. 1	Oklahoma State	Away	Win	53-0

Final ranking: AP, 1st; UPI, 1st

1957 (10-1)
Big Seven Champions

Date	Opponent	Site	Result	Score
Sept. 21	Pittsburgh	Away	Win	26-0
Oct. 5	Iowa State	Home	Win	40-14
Oct. 12	Texas	Dallas	Win	21-7
Oct. 19	Kansas	Home	Win	34-12
Oct. 26	Colorado	Home	Win	14-13
Nov. 2	Kansas State	Away	Win	13-0
Nov. 9	Missouri	Away	Win	39-14
Nov. 16	Notre Dame	Home	Loss	0-7
Nov. 23	Nebraska	Away	Win	32-7
Nov. 30	Oklahoma State	Home	Win	53-6
Jan. 1	Duke (Orange Bowl)		Win	48-21

Final ranking: AP, 4th; UPI, 4th

1958 (10-1)
Big Eight Champions

Date	Opponent	Site	Result	Score
Sept. 27	West Virginia	Home	Win	47-14
Oct. 4	Oregon	Home	Win	6-0
Oct. 11	Texas	Dallas	Loss	14-15
Oct. 18	Kansas	Away	Win	43-0
Oct. 25	Kansas State	Home	Win	40-6
Nov. 1	Colorado	Away	Win	23-7
Nov. 8	Iowa State	Away	Win	20-0
Nov. 15	Missouri	Home	Win	39-0
Nov. 22	Nebraska	Home	Win	40-7
Nov. 29	Oklahoma State	Away	Win	7-0

Final ranking: AP, 5th; UPI, 5th

1959 (7-3)
Big Eight Champions

Date	Opponent	Site	Result	Score
Sept. 26	Northwestern	Away	Loss	13-45
Oct. 3	Colorado	Home	Win	42-12
Oct. 10	Texas	Dallas	Loss	12-19
Oct. 17	Missouri	Away	Win	23-0
Oct. 24	Kansas	Home	Win	7-6
Oct. 31	Nebraska	Away	Loss	21-25
Nov. 7	Kansas State	Away	Win	36-0
Nov. 14	Army	Home	Win	28-20
Nov. 21	Iowa State	Home	Win	35-12
Nov. 28	Oklahoma State	Home	Win	17-7

Final ranking: AP, NR; UPI, 17th

1960 (3-6-1)

Date	Opponent	Site	Result	Score
Sept. 24	Northwestern	Home	Loss	3-19
Oct. 1	Pittsburgh	Home	Win	15-14
Oct. 8	Texas	Dallas	Loss	0-24
Oct. 15	Kansas	Away	Tie	13-13
Oct. 22	Kansas State	Home	Win	49-7
Oct. 29	Colorado	Away	Loss	0-7
Nov. 5	Iowa State	Away	Loss	6-10
Nov. 12	Missouri	Home	Loss	19-41
Nov. 19	Nebraska	Home	Loss	14-17
Nov. 26	Oklahoma State	Away	Win	17-6

Final ranking: NR

1961 (5-5)

Date	Opponent	Site	Result	Score
Sept. 30	Notre Dame	Away	Loss	6-19
Oct. 7	Iowa State	Home	Loss	15-21
Oct. 14	Texas	Dallas	Loss	7-28
Oct. 21	Kansas	Home	Loss	0-10
Oct. 28	Colorado	Home	Loss	14-22
Nov. 4	Kansas State	Away	Win	17-6
Nov. 11	Missouri	Away	Win	7-0
Nov. 18	Army	Yankee Stadium	Win	14-8
Nov. 25	Nebraska	Away	Win	21-14
Dec. 2	Oklahoma State	Home	Win	21-13

Final ranking: NR

1962 (8-3)
Big Eight Champions

Date	Opponent	Site	Result	Score
Sept. 22	Syracuse	Home	Win	7-3
Sept. 29	Notre Dame	Home	Loss	7-13
Oct. 13	Texas	Dallas	Loss	6-9
Oct. 20	Kansas	Away	Win	13-7
Oct. 27	Kansas State	Home	Win	47-0
Nov. 3	Colorado	Away	Win	62-0
Nov. 10	Iowa State	Away	Win	41-0
Nov. 17	Missouri	Home	Win	13-0
Nov. 24	Nebraska	Home	Win	34-6
Dec. 1	Oklahoma State	Away	Win	37-6
Jan. 1	Alabama (Orange Bowl)		Loss	0-17

Final ranking: AP, 8th; UPI, 7th

1963 (8-2)

Date	Opponent	Site	Result	Score
Sept. 21	Clemson	Home	Win	31-14
Sept. 28	Southern Cal	Away	Win	17-12
Oct. 12	Texas	Dallas	Loss	7-28
Oct. 19	Kansas	Home	Win	21-18
Oct. 26	Kansas State	Away	Win	34-9
Nov. 2	Colorado	Home	Win	35-0
Nov. 9	Iowa State	Home	Win	35-0
Nov. 16	Missouri	Away	Win	13-3
Nov. 23	Nebraska	Away	Loss	20-29
Nov. 30	Oklahoma State	Home	Win	34-10

Final ranking: AP, 10th; UPI, 8th

Saint Louis Cardinals Coaching Record
1978 (6-10)

Date	Opponent	Site	Result	Score
Sept. 3	Chicago Bears	Away	Loss	10-17
Sept. 10	New England Patriots	Home	Loss	6-16
Sept. 17	Washington Redskins	Home	Loss	10-28
Sept. 24	Dallas Cowboys	Away	Loss	12-21
Oct. 1	Miami Dolphins	Away	Loss	10-24
Oct. 8	Baltimore Colts	Home	Loss	17-30
Oct. 15	Dallas Cowboys	Home	Loss	21-24 (OT)
Oct. 22	New York Jets	Away	Loss	10-23
Oct. 29	Philadelphia Eagles	Away	Win	16-10
Nov. 5	New York Giants	Home	Win	20-10
Nov. 12	San Francisco 49ers	Away	Win	16-10
Nov. 19	Washington Redskins	Away	Win	27-17
Nov. 26	Philadelphia Eagles	Home	Loss	10-14
Dec. 3	Detroit Lions	Home	Win	21-14
Dec. 10	New York Giants	Away	Loss	0-17
Dec. 17	Atlanta Falcons	Home	Win	42-21

1979 (5-11)
(3-10 under Wilkinson,
2-1 under interim coach Larry Wilson)

Date	Opponent	Site	Result	Score	
Sept. 2	Dallas Cowboys	Home	Loss	21-22	
Sept. 9	New York Giants	Away	Win	27-14	
Sept. 16	Pittsburgh Steelers	Home	Loss	21-24	
Sept. 23	Washington Redskins	Home	Loss	7-17	
Sept. 30	Los Angeles Rams	Away	Loss	0-21	
Oct. 7	Houston Oilers	Away	Win	24-17	
Oct. 14	Philadelphia Eagles	Home	Loss	20-24	
Oct. 21	Dallas Cowboys	Away	Loss	13-22	
Oct. 28	Cleveland Browns	Home	Loss	20-38	
Nov. 4	Minnesota Vikings	Home	Win	37-7	
Nov. 11	Washington Redskins	Away	Loss	28-30	
Nov. 18	Philadelphia Eagles	Away	Loss	13-16	
Nov. 25	Cincinnati Bengals	Away	Loss	28-34	
Dec. 2	San Francisco 49ers	Home	Win	13-10	(Wilson)
Dec. 9	New York Giants	Home	Win	29-20	(Wilson)
Dec. 16	Chicago Bears	Away	Loss	6-42	(Wilson)

INDEX